# THE NEW MILLIONAIRE'S HANDBOOK

## A GUIDE TO CONTEMPORARY SOCIAL CLIMBING

Chris Fountain

Andrews McMeel
Publishing

Kansas City

00 01 02 03 04 RDH 10 9 8 7 6 5 4 3 2 1

Library of Congress Cataloging-in-Publication Data

Fountain, Chris.
The new millionaire's handbook : a guide to contemporary
social climbing / Chris Fountain.
   p. cm.
ISBN 0-7407-1167-9 (pbk.)
   1. United States—Social life and customs—1971—Humor. 2. Rich
people—Humor. 3. Social skills—Humor. I. Title.

E169.04 .F68 2000
973.92—dc21                                                    00-35511

Book design by Holly Camerlinck

To Nancy Fountain, for tolerating me at varying distances over the past twenty years, and our children, John, Katharine, and Sarah. Despite growing up in Greenwich, guys, you've all turned out to be wonderful human beings. That said, anyone expecting a Gelaendewagen to appear under the Christmas tree this year is doomed to disappointment.

"You can't have a decent social pyramid
without an equally decent shimmer of envy
rising like transparent heat waves from
its base. We wouldn't be here at the top
if they weren't down there at the bottom
and visa [*sic*] versa. Isn't that a lovely vision?"

BARCLAY FRERY, COLUMNIST, *GREENWICH POST,* JANUARY 7, 2000

# CONTENTS

# ACKNOWLEDGMENTS

This book would not have been possible without the assistance of Jane Basham. Special thanks are also due to my early readers and encouragers: Bob Brooks (you'd have received the dedication, Bob, but I think my next book will embarrass you even more), Ann Sweeney, Joel and Jeremy Kaye, Warren Cassell, Howard Fast, Sheila Phelan, and Owen Lock. Deborah Brault, for everything, the First Lutheran Noon Group—you all know who you are, even if I don't, and my agent, Jacques de Spoelberch, who did for me what I could not do for myself: Get me published.

**You've done it.** **Landed on a Wall Street trading desk,** made it through the year, and are about to receive the first in a string of well-deserved annual bonuses, which will be larger than the gross national products of Malaysia and Fiji combined. Or perhaps the Internet company you've been working for has completed its first IPO and you're sitting on vested options. Either way, Lu-Ann's been scouting the suburbs and has narrowed her choice of mansions to three; tomorrow, you'll go with her to make the final selection—you have arrived, big time.

But have you? Do you know what's waiting for you out here, just a few miles from the corporate jungle where you—you tiger you—roam so fearlessly? It's not just crabgrass.

Picture this: you and Lu-Ann are dressed to the nines for your meeting with the Indian Nose Yacht Club's admission committee: Lu-Ann's in a designer dress she saw in *Vogue,* one that amply displays her boisterous bosom, while you're in a Men's Warehouse special that the salesman swore was indistinguishable from a $3,000 Brioni. You pull into the parking lot and notice that you're the only one driving a Corvette, and the stunned crowd flinching at the sound of your glass-packed mufflers doesn't seem to be as friendly as you had hoped. Inside, when Lu-Ann orders a Seven and Seven to accompany your Bud Lite, they all grow quiet in the admissions room while Lu-Ann nervously tugs her (very well done and incredibly expensive) dye job and you stroke your Miami of Ohio booster tie and wonder what's gone wrong. You're rich; they're rich. You're young; the confident people surrounding you are also young. But you're flopping about and gasping like a dying fish, while when they aren't just ignoring you, they're shooting dismissive glances in your direction. What the hell has happened? What secret code do you lack that would ease you into the secret world of the new elite? Is there someone you can turn to for advice, for a path through the jungle of this alien world of the rich?

Well, of course there is. You are about to meet Whitney Palmer: she's rich, good looking, and knows everything there is to know about our generation of new-breed rich, and, thank God, she's willing to tell you about it. Whit's a full-metal-jacketed member of the New Generation: Episcopal preschool, Miss Porter's Academy, and a brief period as a scholar at Rhodes (Rhodes College, Tennessee—Whitney's far too smart to intimidate men by displaying a muscular brain). A Salomon Brothers bond trader at twenty-three, she's been a suburban mommy for the past ten years. She now devotes her time to the Junior League and the Historical Society and has led the Hospital Charity Auction for the past five years. She bought her first Hermès Kelly Bag at twelve (when her father gave her her first credit card), she was eating egg-white omelettes and snapping at waiters by fourteen, and she has a collection of cell phones in every color. She dines with Susie Hilfiger, summers in East Hampton, and has weekend homes in all five of the top locations. To my knowledge, Whitney was the first to send her dry cleaning to Paris, thereby incurring $6,000 monthly cleaning bills and the absolute topper in the "How can I possibly spend all my money?" game. In short, the girl lives the life we all aspire to; she knows her world, and she knows everybody who is anybody in that world.

As our better suburbs grew from small towns peopled by simple fox hunters and art collectors to mini-metropoli swarming with new arrivals like you and me, the original settlers despaired at the degradation of their way of life. In California they've labeled us PUKEs–Prosperous, Ungrateful, Kid Entrepreneurs–and in the rest of the country we're called RATs, for Rich, Arrogant Tricycle motors. Either way, the message is the same: we don't belong out here in the suburbs, according to the Old Money farts. Summit, New Jersey; Darien, Connecticut; Chestnut Hill, Massachusetts; Napa Valley; and even dreadful places in the Midwest and South like Fargo and Savannah have all been infested by us, at a rate which proves that the tax brackets are no longer doing their intended job of separating Old Money from the masses.

The dog barks, but the caravan moves on. These snobbish Preps can't bar our entry–who else would buy their grandfather's estate at the price we're willing to pay?–and today we outnumber them by a factor of thousands. We're younger, much better looking, and far, far richer than everyone whose robber baron ancestor's wealth has been watered down over three generations. So, having conquered, why are we still so insecure? Why do we think that Old Money is better than New? Why, when we discipline one of our servants for clumsily dropping the dish of Chateaubriand, do we cringe at our guests' sneers? Does Prep still rule? Must we be civil to people, even when we're paying them? Can't we throw a temper tantrum in front of store clerks? What was the point of getting rich?

Don't worry, Prep is dead, and now we're free to do whatever our black hearts and fiery emotions suggest. We're entitled to the respect that has always been awarded to the rich, and we *Demand* it! *Now!* That said, there are still, sadly, a few rules that must be followed. These rules are different from the rules delineated in the old, now-outdated *Official Preppy Handbook* of two decades ago, because today we do not hide our wealth, and we certainly don't strive to achieve that endearing, shabby gentility Preps were so proud of. What we need is an up-to-date guide, one that delineates the new rules in easy-to-understand language. Once we've learned and conformed to them, we can all relax and enjoy our new wealth. The Prep has started on the long road to oblivion, banished forever to the moldy lawns of Deerfield. He and his pals may still drive battered Volvos to Newport and wear duct-taped Top-Siders and L. L. Bean barn jackets, but the rest of us have been freed to display the wealth that is so reflective of our inner worth. Masters of the world, revolt: you have nothing to lose except a frayed wardrobe. To quote that old clergyman, "Free at last, free at last. Thank God Almighty, we're free at last."

So what are these rules? Who will set them down in a nicely illustrated guide, broken down into brief paragraphs so as not to tax our attention span? The problem once defined, I thought immediately of Whitney, and this book is the result of that dear girl's enthusiastic response.

# Chapter 1

# TO THE SUBURBS

# WEALTH

There was a time, long ago, when the upper class hid its wealth. Understatement was the leitmotif of all public appearance, in dress, housing, and transportation. Old was cherished, new shunned, and no one ever admitted to being truly wealthy. This is no longer the case.

Today, the denizens of La Jolla, Birmingham (Michigan, darling), and Charleston shout out their riches. We of the New Order wallow in our money, roll in it, fling it into the air, and scream, "Look at me!" Our celebration is an ongoing public orgasmic frenzy that must be joined in by all: to refuse is to invite condemnation and banishment from the new society, for nobody likes the cheese who stands alone.

Our new generation is generous—we're all folks who will gladly give you our last Havana if you will only permit us to tell you how much it cost—but we are strangely insecure about our worth as human beings. As our wealth poured in so unexpectedly in the late eighties, and then continued into the nineties, we were at first amazed at our good fortune and a little unsure about how long it would last. Then, when no one showed up to claim it, we settled down a bit, uncertain about what to do with all this cash but certain that we deserved it. We battled our insecurity by banding together into our own neighborhoods, where everyone around us earns the same enormous amounts and everyone takes the same kind of vacations. We don't read, we don't vote, but every one of us can tell an eager listener exactly what a Rolex Oyster (or a Block Island oyster) costs, and can discuss the relative merits of heli-skiing in Crested Butte versus the Abercrombie & Kent tour of Patagonia. We're all much more comfortable now. You will want to join us here.

# Chapter 2

# THE PROPER HOME

# REAL ESTATE

Much of our wealth is invested in real estate: primary homes, weekend getaways, and vacation estates. Just as every Kansan can happily quote you the current silo price for wheat, members of our class are expected to and do know the real estate market in every town they own property in. Training begins early; play dates between six-year-olds are frequently disrupted by squabbles over whose foundation footprint is larger and whether to include the pool house in square-footage calculations. By ten, and continuing throughout our adulthood, we must know the market value of each house on our street, the relative pricing of each neighborhood, and be fluently conversant on the latest Big Deals. Once we're initiated, up-to-date knowledge is transmitted by osmosis, but newcomers will want to spend a few days being coached by their real estate agent. Don't neglect this important area of learning or, when you do move in and are invited to your first cocktail party, you will have nothing to talk to anyone about.

All right: ready? Finished your training? Flexed those brain cells? Then we're ready to leave the city and find our new home.

# NEIGHBORHOODS

No town is a monolith, although New Canaan comes close. Buy in the right town but the wrong neighborhood and you will be automatically barred from the best clubs and schools. A modest bungalow in one of the proper neighborhoods is worth far more in social acceptance than the largest mansion in a less desirable one. A newcomer can't tell which is which, because outward appearances are not determinative. Your only contact in your target town, your sole hope of being placed in the correct area and getting into the right clubs is your real estate agent. You simply can't rely on "For Sale" signs. If such commercial signage is permitted at all, it exists only on the lawns of houses worth less than a million dollars, and only in unacceptable areas of town. No, you must use the services of a real estate broker and, unfortunately, her first interest is in preserving her livelihood by keeping up the standards of her town. If she believes you're the sort to store a bass boat and trailer on your driveway, you will be shown nothing but waterfront mansions down the street from the dump.

You must convince the woman—and every newly single mother in the suburbs peddles real estate (see "Divorce," in chapter 13)— that you and Lu-Ann are worthy of the better neighborhoods, and this convincing must begin the first time she interviews you. Here are some tips for that all-important meeting:

Leave the kids back in the apartment with their nanny.

Ditch the Corvette—you can't have one in the suburbs—and rent or buy the most expensive Mercedes available. Whatever you find, your agent's will be larger, but you don't want to be seriously shown up in this area.

Throw in your gold jewelry when you sell the 'Vette.

Change Lu-Ann's name to something more suitable for your new environment; see our list of names in the Appendix for ideas.

# ESTATES

You didn't move to the suburbs to live in a squatter's cottage of, say, five thousand square feet. You need more space than that—far more. A four-car garage is the minimum, and it must be accompanied by at least five bedrooms, six baths, a great room, a cherry-paneled library (for home-entertainment equipment, not books), and several playrooms: one for the adults and reserved for formal occasions only and two, at minimum, for the children—one off the kitchen, where the dog will live, and one upstairs so that the teens can entertain their friends in privacy. You will require a cigar room, wine cellar, simulated trading room, and a separate servants' wing. The "library" must have a projection TV built into the furniture or dropping from the ceiling, at least one fireplace, and that felicitous combination of hideous design, cost, and discomfort that only a professional decorator can provide. The full mini-theater, with stadium seating and plush arm chairs, is best contained in a separate "media room."

Suburban life is not intended to be a *Little House on the Prairie* experience, so be sure to build enough house that your acreage doesn't overwhelm you. Properly sited and sized, a thirty-thousand-square-foot house can provide a nice sense of crowded community even on a ten-acre lot. Build close to the property line or, better yet, property line to property line, and get ready to meet your new neighbors—but don't forget to leave enough space for the circular Belgian-block driveway.

There are two distinct housing types in our suburbs, and depending on your age, either one will suit you perfectly.

### Training Mansions

You are twenty-four years old, just out of UCLA and starting your career in Silicon Valley. You need a house to make a statement, of course, but the $10 million mansions are out of reach for another two or even (bear markets happen!) three years. What to do?

Fortunately, builders have addressed and answered this problem for you, and training mansions, also known as starter mansions or even McMansions™, are now available in all of the better suburbs. These are modest homes, generally costing no more than $3 or $4 million, but they afford the young homeowner an opportunity to practice now the skills he will need on the larger estate he so richly deserves. Your wife, Jennifer, will have six to seven thousand square feet to decorate and you, Cooper, can oversee a small band of illegal yard workers in preparation for the army you'll need when you move up; each of you will get a feel for what's required to manage a great estate.

You won't be living in extreme conditions, of course. Our generation has produced builders who know exactly what we need, so the master bath will have the requisite marble whirlpool, the bidet, the glass enclosed and atrium-ceilinged shower (with five or six oversized chrome showerheads), his and her vanities and sinks, and so forth. The kitchen will dwarf even the master bath but, while the ubiquitous commercial gas range will be present, the cabinets won't be top-of-the-line custom work. And, sadly, your yard will be just a smidgeon too small to properly serve its function of announcing to the world, "Here is one who truly matters." Training mansions are merely a side track on the railroad of life, but don't worry: because you are the exceptional person that you are, you'll be back on the main track shortly, and ready to move forward to bigger and therefore better things, like:

## Whopper Mansions

These are reserved for those who have truly arrived: top traders, Silicon Valley PUKEs, movie stars, and the more tradi-

tional trust-fund babies. A whopper is just what the name implies: one giant, "Who's got the biggest balls on the block?" chunk of lumber and stone, all served up on a minimum of five acres of fescue. Usually built on the site of a $3 to $10 million "tear down," a thirty-thousand-square-foot whopper shouts to the world that, God damn it, you've arrived, you're here, and you've got the best bankruptcy lawyers in the country on retainer to make sure you stay here. There are, and can be, no standards of taste for these behemoths—so long as all furnishings are hideously expensive and clearly marked as such—all will be well. Nonetheless, there are rules governing their construction and use. These are set forth in the following chapters.

# Chapter 3

# FINE-TUNING YOUR ENVIRONMENT

# EXTERIORS

Proper attention to the exterior of your home will ensure a smooth reception from your new neighbors. We judge by appearances in the suburbs, and the appearance of your home tells us who you are and, more importantly, what your effect will be on our property values.

## Stone Walls, Never Fences

The new suburbanite insists on stone walls guarding him from the street, and no wonder! These creations are maintenance-free and yet wonderfully expensive, so no one will accuse you of stinting in this most important area of your home. Stone walls assert your ownership and declare your ability to protect what is yours in a stern, unyielding manner that no wooden fence can ever aspire to.

## Gates

Stone walls writ ornate. An unguarded driveway is an open admission that the owner within has nothing better to do than entertain unan-

nounced visitors, while a gate demands recognition that behind them resides a very busy person indeed. Your gate will be iron or steel, naturally. Some of us like to retreat to gated communities where trained personnel confront visitors for us, but the classic combination of rock and steel provides a very nice gated community of one in areas where the surrounding community just doesn't share our values.

### Exterior Lighting

There's no sense constructing tens of thousands of square feet of great rooms and billiard parlors if it's all blocked from view by the ten-foot wall you constructed; this is where exterior lighting comes in. Your house, properly designed, will tower over even the tallest of rock piles, and searchlights beamed on its upper reaches will serve as a beacon of your arrival to all who pass by.

## Renovating

Redecorating must be done seasonally; complete renovations are performed every three years. No suburban home is complete without a green Dumpster parked in its driveway, for it implies that you are about to begin yet another improvement. For those of you temporarily overextended, this subterfuge can work for quite a while: announce that you've switched architects again, and you can keep them guessing forever.

Whom do we use for our renovations? Not Sal and his pickup, God forbid, and certainly not one of those dreadful "design and-contract-all-in-one" firms from poorer regions of our state. The local hot architects (check your society magazine for names and pictures) are called in for consultations and then, after you've mentioned all the candidates at your club and learned which one is "hottest" that week, a contract is signed. After an appropriate waiting period, your architect will put out his plans for bid, and you will receive three quotes, each at least double your original mental budget. The builders, who generally favor doeskin slippers when off the construction site, will visit your home to interview the entire family, including pets. If all of you pass muster, one or even two of the firms will consent to do the job, sometime in the next twenty-four months. Each is well qualified—they work only on the very best houses in town—but choosing between them need not be a chore. Again, your club contacts will help you learn who has the preferred name, and then—voila!—your construction job begins, three months after the promised start date and continuing long past the date contracted for finish. You must not worry; the Dumpsters sprawled across the lawn will convey the proper impression of an expensive and extensive project (and a renovation project requiring less than six months to complete is no reno-

## Power Nesting

Power Nesting is the latest craze to hit the suburbs, and you will want to join in the fun. It is no longer enough to tear down a $7 million house "because it just doesn't work for us"—you must accomplish the renovation in a nanosecond, and you must make sure that your friends are aware of this miraculous (and expensive, of course) foreshortening of time. You can, if you are willing and able to hire fifty contractors with hundreds of workers, buy a house on Memorial Day and have it completely gutted and renovated by the Fourth of July. This will cost you at least five times what a regularly paced redo would, but that's the point! Plus, the less patience we display, the more important we must be.

vation at all, and must never even be mentioned to one's peers).

Nitpickers can relax. There is absolutely no correlation between quality carpentry and market resale value in the suburbs, for new homes or used. Knotty pine may be substituted for the specified clear No. 1 trim, walls may bow, and bathrooms may be vented into a nearby closet, but no one will care and you won't lose a penny on your investment. In fact, in a bow to modernity, builders are now gluing together prefabricated monsters complete with faux-marble counters and warped flooring and still demanding up to $5 million for their creations. They get it, too.

## Lawn Maintenance

We do not own lawn mowers in the suburbs. We never do our own yardwork, nor do we try to hire a local teenager to do that work for us (not that he'd accept the job anyway). We do employ teams of illegal aliens to sweep our yards of debris and keep drives and pathways free of snow. True story: R. "Press" Worthington woke up one warm spring Saturday and decided, after finishing off that week's *Barron's,* to tool up to the end of his very long driveway on his rider tractor and trim an overhanging bit of shrubbery. His cell phone rang just as he returned to his garage and, answering it, he heard his neighbor say, "Here in the Lakespur District we do *not* attend to our own landscaping, nor do we permit our professional gardeners to operate machinery on weekends. I don't expect to *ever* have to make this sort of call again." Click.

Press was lucky it was a lady calling; her husband might simply have run him over with his Range Rover. Don't let this happen to you.

## Pools

Even in Nebraska, no rectangular pool is acceptable (and for those of you who have truly just arrived, we'll point out, surely needlessly, that above-ground pools are reserved for trailer-park recreation centers). Your home must be adorned with a free-form, custom-designed wonder, lined with Gunite™ or Pebble Tec™, and surrounded by faced stone—never tile. You will want the latest fiber-optic lighting system and heating, of course, and the entire package will nestle in a jewel-like setting of exotic plantings and deep, weed-free lawn. Although you may never intend to swim in it, your pool will provide an indispensable anchor for your landscape design, so grab that checkbook and start digging!

Lap pools, in case you do actually swim, are permissible in the suburbs, but they are best built indoors, near or in the private gym.

## Golf Courses

We have our club for escaping wives and children on weekends, but what whispers loud, boastful assurance better than a putting green and a one-hole course, set amid our own private acreage? Locate your gem within sight of the pool, nestled into the rolling hills your designer (Trent Jones or Jack Nicholas) will create for you. Here will be the perfect place for little Courtney and Trevor to begin their training in this essential social grace.

## Outdoor Cooking Centers

Formerly known as "barbecue grills," these new suburban wonders will impress your friends and leave them bewitched with envy, at least until they buy one of their own—after that, you'll all have fun racing each other to the top of the category. All our better kitchen suppliers make cooking centers, but Viking, Frontgate, and Benson will offer the price range you're interested in: $4,500 to $9,950—any more, and you'll be nearing that fine line which demarcates necessity from excessiveness. And, after all, as it is the catering staff who will be the ones actually firing these monsters up, how much convenience do you really need?

You will want a professional model, one made from sixteen-gauge stainless steel and offering at least six burners, each firing at 15,000 BTUs. That's 90,000 BTUs of total scorching power, and that's a lot! The stove must burn propane or natural gas, as well as charcoal and hardwood, and include an infrared rotisserie, granite counters, a built-in oven, 110 volts, GFI outlets), and weigh a minimum of 750 pounds, not including accessories.

What accessories are "must haves"? Plenty. A pair of weatherproof, halogen grill lights, restaurant heat lamps, Texas-sized stockpots, a traditional turkey fryer (ask your retailer), a smoking-chamber system, a freestanding domed masonry pizza oven (wood-fired, of course) matched with an outdoor hearth (with protective screen—remember the children!), personalized branding irons for those steaks, an electric ice shaver, stainless steel torches, Sno-Kone® machine, electric ice cream/sorbet chest, stainless steel commercial straw dispenser, professional chef's jacket (to wear while overseeing the help), and so forth (whew!). Let your imagination run wild here; you can never overaccessorize.

Don't forget, your open-air entertainment system just won't be complete without a professional beverage-service center. Typically built from Type 304 stainless steel, these wheeled beauties come with all the essentials: an insulated ice compartment, chilling well, four-bottle speed rail, plumbed sink (use a garden hose and water filter if necessary, but except in the South or Texas, this may be considered tacky with a capital $T$), polypropylene cutting board, and bottle opener. Need more? Just ask—the companies who provide these sorts of amenities just *love* serving you!

# INTERIORS

*"People need to be shown how to live."*

−RALPH LAUREN

### Furnishings and Decorating

Most of us hire the services of an interior decorator (and that decorator will be named something like Penelope Langdon-Smith or we might just as well save our money) to make certain that we pay absolute top dollar for our flocked wallpaper and artwork, but some may prefer to be stolen from personally, face to face, by antique dealers and upholstery salesmen. Either approach is fine, so long as one errs on the side of excess. Remember, "architects don't do charm anymore," so just relax when you end up with a "French/Georgian contemporary" with industrial-sized appliances. As one proud owner of just such a creation told the *New York Times,* "It's that eclectic look." You betcha!

The suburbs are known among the cognoscenti as swamplands of dubiously pedigreed antiques and paintings. This is not our fault; we didn't grow up with the stuff, for Christ's sake, so how would we distinguish between a genuine New England oak night-soil receptacle and a knockoff manufactured from Malaysian baobab wood? Or a

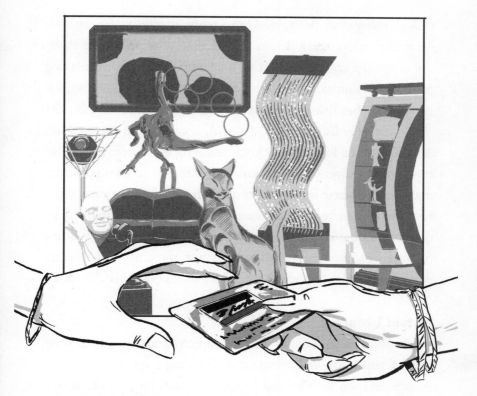

genuine Degas from a "Doug," painted by our interior decorator's struggling nephew? We can't, and we don't have to. Simply turn your charge card over to the decorator and relax. Your friends use her services too, so they will be certain to have other works by Doug in their homes. Your Dougs will have cost just as *much* as a Degas, and by golly, that's good enough!

## Books

Rarely a problem with new construction, many purchasers of used housing are confronted with acres of floor-to-ceiling bookshelves, left over from a different time. We have all seen the pitiful attempts of hapless amateurs who try to fill this space, but there are only so many duck decoys and brass naval timepieces one can stick on a shelf before being driven mad. The sensible solution is to rip the things out entirely and create a new book collection consisting of just five volumes: a Monet coffee-table volume of water lilies, the current number one fiction and nonfiction titles from the *New York Times* best-seller lists, a spiritual-growth book such as *Oh, the Places You'll Go!*, and a local history book featuring the "Great Estates" in town, with a silver-plated bookmark marking your own particular mansion (a discrete inquiry to the publisher will usually yield a special edition with your house pasted in—worth every penny!). "The carpenter doing the renovations asked if I wanted to save a few bookshelves," one perplexed suburbanite mommy was recently overheard saying, "but what would I do with a bookshelf?" Exactly.

### Instant Libraries

Sometimes the built-in shelving of an old mansion is such an integral part of the architecture that removing it is impossible. Our decorators used to solve this problem by installing "books by the yard": six yards of blue bindings, four of green, and so on. The homeowner ended up with three thousand volumes of Reader's Digest Condensed Books, and this caused some embarrassment when, once a decade, a literate guest actually read the titles. The new solution uses *real* books—leather-bound, gold lettering, and all that. For $50,000 and up, a personal library dealer will assemble an "instant library" made up of antiquarian titles on such deep subjects as Roman history, Greek philosophy, and even Xenophon's *Anabasis*. One such dealer says, wistfully, "These books are pretty and decorative looking, but hopefully, the client will pick one up one day." Not likely, but your shelves will certainly impart the look of a finely honed brain, and won't *that* be impressive!

Buying books in this fashion not only means that you will set just the right tone for your "library"; it's a real time-saver, too. Mrs. Ginnie Maxcopf recently moved into her new home in Savannah and found the task of filling acres of bookshelves with knickknacks and best-sellers awfully daunting. "I just didn't have the time," wailed this stay-at-home mom, "between play dates and shopping, and besides, buying books one by one would be, like, such a total waste of time! So I called up my decorator and bam! Within two weeks every shelf was filled with really marvelous titles. It's so cool!" Indeed it is, Ginnie.

## Magazines

We may not do much in the way of books in the suburbs, but we make up for that in our careful use of magazines. Here are just some of the better publications we will want to display:

*Vogue, W, Country Life* (we're all Anglophiles—the one holdover from days of Prepdom), the local society press or 'the Swells' magazine, *Yachting* (regardless of the proximity of your home to a coastline—it implies the existence of a coastal weekend home), *Polo, Architectural Digest, Southern Accents, Town & Country, Match,* and *Gray's Sporting Journal* (not *Field & Stream,* for heaven's sake!). Scatter a few Abercrombie & Kent and Equitour brochures about your coffee tables and powder rooms and you'll set just the right tone. *People* magazine is kept in your master bedroom, under the mattress—after all, you learn all the news about the important people firsthand, don't you?

## Kitchens

You will be tempted to skip this section, as the new suburbanite does not cook, but do so at your peril! The kitchen is the ultimate statement room, and you must have a big one, regardless of your culinary skills or interest. It will be designed by a specialist, never the general architect, and must include two side-by-side Sub-Zero stainless steel refrigerators, additional refrigerated drawers underneath the English "bespoke" cabinetry (Christopher Peacock made-to-order is best), three stainless steel sinks (with goosenecked faucets), two center islands, and a Viking or Garland commercial stove. The sky's the limit on this latter item, but any stove costing between $50,000 and $100,000 should produce the desired effect.

Granite countertops and handmade, Mexican ceramic floor tiles still prevail, despite the efforts of certain effete designers to move on. Corian remains a cheap imitation of the real thing, and you do not ever want to be accused of cheapness in this, the show-case of your home. Hardwood flooring, while daring, may be safely substituted for peasant tiles, and a freestanding butcher block will

contrast nicely with the stone counters. French copper omelette pans hanging by the triple-sized windows imply that you've completed your chef's tour of Provence.

You may place bar setups by one of the sinks, if you wish, so that you'll have an opportunity to use this lovely room. And, of course, don't forget the adjoining butler's pantry (with yet another dishwasher) between the kitchen and the dining room—we must never live in a house with a direct passage to or from the kitchen. In the pantry or behind the bar, you'll want a commercial ice maker that produces "designer ice": perfectly formed, clear wafers of ice so different from the irregular, cloudy cubes served to the hoi polloi. Once again, Sub-Zero is your friend here, offering a modestly priced ($1,875) cuber to sit beside its $4,500 wine chiller. If you must spend more, or if the sixty-pound daily output of the Sub-Zero is inadequate, U-Line, Marvel, and Scotsman all have models to suit your refined demands.

## Appliances

European only: Miele and Asko are best You won't actually use these, of course—that's what maids are for—but no $600 GE dishwasher can possibly give your kitchen the same luster as two side-by-side, $1,500 Mieles. The same reasoning dictates your choice of washing machines, dryers, and vacuums.

## The Private Gym

The subject of exercise is too important to bury in a subchapter, so we will discuss it later on. For now, know that your mansion must have at least one gym, and preferably two, where your guests can admire StairMasters, weights (for the ladies, these will come in bright, cheerful colors like pink or baby blue),

NordicTrack machines, and the like. These rooms will always include separate baths with whirlpools and saunas, even though Mom does most of her exercise at the admission-only training club under the watchful eye of Oskar the Austrian.

### The Powder Room

A very, very large room with a very small Picasso will nicely set the tone here. Add custom wallpaper, monogrammed hand towels, and Caswell-Masey scented soap balls.

### Children's Bathrooms

Each of your gifted progeny must have her own. Your bathroom designer can help out here, but the essentials include a whirlpool for soaking after field hockey, vast amounts of counter space (if you must economize, Corian can be substituted for granite), a linen closet, a tanning bed, a computer, and a telephone.

### The Master Bath

"The new bathroom is a fully furnished, fully decorated sitting room that just happens to have a bathtub in the middle and a toilet in a closet," says Barclay Smithers, noted Marin County decorator. The only other difference is size: sitting rooms are smaller.

Next to your kitchen, the most important statement room in your house is your master bath. It must be decorated with antiques and hold a whirlpool, sauna, and steam bath, a glassed-in shower with multiple showerheads, a regular soaking tub at least eight feet long and five feet wide, exercise equipment (including a StairMaster and free weights), a mini-kitchen with separate sink, microwave, refrigerator, and coffeemaker, and, in a private area, a state of the art toilet. Television, telephone, computer workstation, juice bar, and top-of-the-line audio go without saying, of course. You will want a fireplace.

Optional accessories can include crystal chandelier lighting, atriums, and goldfish ponds. For privacy from the outside, you may wish to add a mini-waterfall that cascades down your wall-to-ceiling windows at appropriate moments. One designer likes to place a chaise lounge, covered in hand-painted silk, in each of her bathroom creations. So impractical, such a loud boast of wealth! Have fun and enjoy!

## Saltwater Aquariums

Everyone must have one of these. Starting at $80,000 or so (plus $500 per month for third-party maintenance—don't tempt your hungry staff!), these thousand-gallon wonders will no longer amaze your friends—after all, they have one, too—but will keep you up to date. Where do these expensive ($1,500 and up) fish come from? That's the best part: poison. Third World fisherman douse a coral reef with cyanide, killing all of the coral and 90 percent of the fish, and send the remaining 10 percent to our shores. Most of the poor dears die en route, sickened as they are, but that just means that the ones who do make it are so much rarer. Rare is exclusive, and exclusive is best. When, a few years from now, there aren't any wild fish left, imagine what an impression your own collection will make. You'll be a regular Jacques Cousteau.

# Chapter 4

# A MOVABLE FEAST: SUBURBAN CARS

Sadly, we can't invite everyone into our home, no matter how large it is! I say sadly because many of our best friendships in the suburbs are made among people who came as visitors and stayed on as friends once they discovered who we were from our furnishings. We'd like to share our values and taste with the entire community, but how can we do that? The answer, of course, is through that magical rolling medium, the automobile. Our cars say every bit as much about us as our clothes, our choice of decorator, and our kitchen. Let's start our introduction to our as-yet-undiscovered friends right, by making sure that our cars represent a seamless transition from our house to our public soul.

## GARAGES

Four-car capacity, minimum. "In Orange County, the attitude is that three-car garages are for poor people." So says the *Wall Street Journal,* and so too will your neighbors in the new suburbs. There is no maximum size, although Jay Leno's forty-four-thousand-square-foot, multilevel wonder might be considered to border on excess anywhere outside of California. You'll want plenty of space to house your twenty-foot Suburban and Excursion, so be sure to have your man measure before committing. Options that really aren't optional include custom-made doors designed to resemble old English horse-stall doors except that they roll up, heating, projection screen, telephone, fax, and computer station. Your home's sound and entertainment system will, of course, extend to this vital structure.

# HOUSEHOLD CARS

Station wagons and then minivans once served as basic wheels to transport the children to the dentist's office and Mom to the club. No more. The proper suburban car must now cost at least $45,000, which rules out all wagons except the Mercedes, and minivans with dog slobber on the windows are a suburban no-no. So are all American cars, with the exception of SUVs, which impart a subtle suggestion of additional houses in ski country and on Nantucket. We do not drive Oldsmobiles in the suburbs, and Cadillacs are reserved for FaFa's retirement in Hobe Sound.

# Mom's and Dad's Cars

The proper car for Mom is a gargantuan four-wheel-drive truck, such as the GMC Suburban, Ford Excursion or Expedition (the Ford Explorer enjoyed its moment in the sun but costs far too little for the proper effect), or any of the expensive imports: Lexus, Range Rover (not a Land Rover—the latter implies that you wanted the Range Rover but couldn't afford it), or, providing it has the leather-seat option, the Toyota Land Cruiser. It is essential that Mother drive one of these behemoths, *even if she has just one child*. Little Lord Fauntleroy may rattle around in back while Mom carts him off to travel soccer, but should she drive a smaller car, her loss in prestige would far outweigh the loneliness of the long-distance passenger. Go big or stay home.

The Hummer is fine for Dad or young Trey (see "Station Cars" and "Children's Cars," below), but not for Mom; its testosterone level overpowers all but the most hard-charging of female executives, and they, of course, don't live in the suburbs.

# The Family Sedan

Even a Suburban can't fill a five-car garage by itself, of course, so it is entirely practical and even expected that the proper family will have a Mercedes sedan for Mom and Dad's evening outings.

We're talking "S" class here; the "E" series nudges the $45,000 barrier but is too small, and we don't consider the baby Mercedes at all unless our au pair is a shrewd bargainer. One exception: the ML320 or its brand-new, larger-engined brother, the 430. The former misses the target price by a hair, and both bear a distressing resemblance to the old AMC Gremlin, but the combination of a Mercedes nameplate and four-wheel drive pull these otherwise ugly beasts into acceptability as either a children's car or Mom's secondary transportation.

# STATION CARS

A lucky few of us reach the city by helicopter, especially you Texans, but it is still permissible to commute by train, for it demonstrates a charming humility and sets an example for the little shaver to follow in his own path through life. Done with the proper noblesse oblige style, commuting by mass transit can be an energizing way to start and end the day. To get to the station, a variety of cars can be considered.

Porsche and BMW each manufacture fine statements of success. Maserati does not; it sounds Italian and, therefore, ephemeral and moody. But you needn't restrict yourself to sports cars when there are so many other suitable choices available, including the Hummer, a Gelaendewagen (Tommy Hilfiger has one, why don't you?), almost any Volvo less than three years old, an Audi, or even a Saab, if it's a convertible. You've earned your money—go out and show people you're enjoying it!

Those of us who grew up in the suburbs may remember when chief executives rode battered one-speed bicycles or drove rusting, rumbling station wagons to the train, and we may be tempted to resurrect that tradition. Try not to. Limousines transport those executives now, and the only old cars at the station belong to out-of-town commuters who have stopped by to boost radios and cell phones. The new suburbs are just that: new, and anything running counter to that image will only cause you difficulties.

# CHILDREN'S CARS

Good taste and common sense will take you far in this area. A beginning driver should not be entrusted with a six-hundred-horsepower Z-3 roadster; save that treat for her senior graduation present. No, the proper starter car is a safe car: one that will protect your gifted progeny while they learn how to drive after sixteen beers. Hummers are best for this purpose, but frugal families often plan their fleet additions in advance, purchasing a new Gargantua SUV for Mom three years before Suzie's sixteenth birthday. That way, just as it is time for new family wheels, the SUV—handwashed and detailed, of course—will be ready for the battering of a novice driver.

# DRIVERS

We don't drive ourselves to the city for our evening entertainment any more. Limousines are always acceptable, but the less pretentious among us hire an off-duty policeman to chauffeur us in our own Mercedes. He'll follow us from the opera to the restaurant to late-night parties, we'll have the pleasure of mentioning our "driver" all evening, and when we return to the suburbs he will go home to wherever it is that policemen live. Economy with class.

# STICKERS ON CARS

Any political bumper sticker except for the winning local Republican team is forbidden. That is not to say, however, that there isn't room for personal expression that can also serve to preserve status. Here is a sampling of acceptable window-glass stickers:

Prep school decals: Hotchkiss or better—we don't necessarily need to inform the world that Orthwaith is matriculating at the Vernor Reed School for Drug Abusers. And we don't put on the standard sticker available in the school bookstore; always sport the "special" ones, which are obtained only by contributing a specified, substantial sum to the endowment fund.

Ivy League colleges, no matter how mediocre, are always proudly displayed, and bookstore stock is perfectly okay in this instance. If Orthwaith drops out to throw pots in North Carolina, a sticker from an Ivy (the one farthest from your home, to forestall embarrassing moments—"I'm going to New Haven today; how about I drop in on that fine son of yours?") can ease the distraught family through the four years of neighbors' inquiries.

# BEACH PERMITS

Nantucket's are best, regardless of which area of our proud country you live in, but whichever you choose, here's a tip: never place one year's pass on top of another. Those in the know line the passes up on the bumper, like a fighter pilot's kills, to show just how long they've been trekking to their little piece of heaven by the sea. When it's time to replace that SUV, careful work with a razor blade (or switching bumpers) will ensure that your statement of longevity survives to impress again another day. No Nantucket

home? Not a problem. Anyone can buy these passes, even renters and day-trippers. Those of you with trusted friends who can keep a confidence (they won't live in the suburbs) may even consider asking them to buy permits for you while they're on their own trip to the island.

Nantucket is the most prestigious pass, but Martha's Vineyard will do in a pinch and, for landlubbers, a Stockbridge, Massachusetts, dump permit adds that classic touch of humble understatement so important in the new millennium. Of course, any such admission of humility should always be balanced with an enameled club emblem bolted to the grill.

# EURO-OVALS

Not the real ones, of course—someone may mistake you for an immigrant—but the simulated stickers with obscure initials. Again, Nantucket takes the lead in this category with its "ACK"—the navigational call letters for the local airport. The average driver behind you will assume that you're just back from Auckland, but that's her worry, isn't it, darling?

Don't content yourself with the average ACK badge, however. The original sticker was a special creation, available only to those who contributed to save the Sankaty lighthouse on our island. Because the minimum donation required to get hold of one of these exclusive little gems was quite large, enterprising merchants soon began offering cheaper versions, which neither made mention of the lighthouse nor demanded a king's ransom to be forked over to the lighthouse folks. Now the poor Yellow-Bellied Sneetches pick up a sticker from the drugstore, slap it on the back of their Suburban, and think that they're passing as Blue-Bellied Sneetches. Don't you make that mistake: you want the original, authentic oval, the one with ACK in big, black letters and "Save Our Sankaty, Inc." in tiny red lettering below. It's doubly obscure, and sends a message to those in the know that you, very clearly, are not a Yellow-Bellied Sneetch.

The oval market is expanding and now includes products proclaiming, for instance, GR. An explanatory footnote hastens to point out that the reference is to Greenwich, not Greece, but why take the chance of such potentially devastating confusion? Stick with the East Coast islands. Or, if you must break free of the crowd and feel a little daring, send a modest contribution to the Bedford, New York, fire department and receive in return an oval stating BFD. A bit risqué for most of our gang.

Vanity plates are to be eschewed, although HUBRIS on a Porsche is acceptable, as it demonstrates both an Ivy League education and a keen sense of irony.

Club burgees, those enameled medallions displaying your club affiliations and affixed to the grill of your Mercedes, are never in poor taste—assuming, of course, it's a Maidstone organization or better. "Harlem River Boat Club," while exotic, will just not do. Go easy here: your golf, tennis, and yacht clubs are sufficient. Any more and you are being ostentatious. The ultimate in sophisticated modesty? Use just a club parking permit to let the world know who you are. Tasteful and effective.

# ROOF RACKS

Dump that old Sears carrier you used to strap onto the Pontiac. New and fresh today means Thule racks, equipped with as many different sports references as space and width permit: bicycle, skiing, kayak, and Windsurfer racks can all be squeezed on, provided your car (and it will be a Suburban or Excursion) will carry it. You don't tote around the actual sports toy, you understand—aerodynamic considerations forbid it. The point is to suggest that you're *going* to do all these things, just as soon as you have a spare moment.

If, for some reason, a Suburban isn't available (there is a six-month wait for these beloved cars, and the Excursion? Forget it!), you will have to be more selective on which sport of the day is displayed on your roof; a Beemer is only so wide. Ski racks in July are fun, implying as they do that you're soon to depart on an overland trek to Chile, but as in life itself, sometimes hard choices must be made on roof decorations. You detest limits on your behavior;

we know that, and we understand, so here's a fashion tip that bows just a teensy bit to reality but keeps you and your car looking fresh and adventurous all year: switch the accessories around. That's right, run the ski motif for a week or two in June, then a kayak rack (for around-town voyages, an actual kayak with its festive plastic colors makes a wonderful accessory to the rack itself), then biking, and so forth. Fashion with a capital *F*!

## RHINO BARS

These tubular steel wonders are used for clearing unwary bicyclists and redwood trees from your path and are an essential accessory for every SUV. A matte-black finish is best, although the little bit of fashion flare supplied by chrome is always in good taste. You won't actually take your fifteen-

foot-wide, leather-seated Excursion or Suburban anywhere near a dirt road (except on Fishers Island, but those are *very* wide paths); after all, proper suburbanites jet to any destination more than a two-hour drive away. Still, the Rhino Bar will protect you from those pesky concrete planters in your driveway. It also serves to demonstrate your rugged bravery—you're ready for anything, and ready to go!

# Chapter 5

# ESSENTIAL SUBURBAN
# ACCESSORIES
# AND
# LIFESTYLES

# CELL PHONES

You will have many of these, in all different colors. Together with your pager, they will link you to your children and your friends. An indispensable tool for suburban living, a cell phone allows you to stay in your Range Rover while waiting in the pickup line at school and call Victoria, in the Lexus ahead of you, to swap restaurant suggestions, rearrange play dates, and exchange the latest news on divorces. So much fun!

A note to the uninitiated: the cell phones provided by corporations to executive's wives always come in black. Always, that is, unless you call the CIO directly and put him in his place. Sad to say, these people refuse to acknowledge your fashion needs and will rise from their chairs to find you the right color only when prodded by you. The most effective of those prods, delivered incessantly in an ever-increasing whine, is "But all my *friends* have them in different colors."

Regardless of what you've heard, size does matter, and in the case of cellular phones, smaller is better. As each new model shrinks in size, a phone that resembles a half baguette is hopelessly out of date and demonstrates that its owner is, too. You will want a new phone every six months to keep up with technological progress and your friends. Oddly enough, this quest for diminuendo is most prevalent among men. The old locker room exercise of comparing tools has been converted to a public showing of smallness. At business meetings, the men all whip out their phones and display them on the table in front of them. Surreptitious glances quickly determine who has the smallest, and that person is top dog for the day. Of course, the winner's chastened competitors will all be on the Internet until the wee hours of the morning, seeking out and ordering still smaller ones, so victory is fleeting, but that's what keeps us on our toes, and the cell-phone industry booming.

# HIRED HELP

*"Why is it anyone's business how we treat our help?"*

—SOUTHHAMPTON HOSTESS

### Au Pairs and Nannies

Essential to any well-thought-of household, au pairs used to be called "mothers' helpers" and were recruited from the ranks of local high school girls temporarily separated from their boyfriends. That changed when a deluded Bel Air housewife mistakenly thought to add a bit of class to the arrangement by referring to her sub-minimum-wage slave by the French term, *au pair,* which is an anagram for *overpaid.* Wages escalated accordingly.

Currently, au pairs demand weekly salaries that exceed your SUV gas allowance, four nights off, health insurance, paid vacations to the Caribbean island of their choice, and an all-wheel-drive vehicle. Nonetheless, no self-respecting household can be without one, so the smart suburbanite will want to economize if possible, hold her nose, and hire one.

It is absolutely essential that your au pair speak English, even if it's a second language. Some struggling households try to make do by importing young Spanish-speaking women from South or Central America, but the cost in prestige more than offsets the lower salary. A better approach is to recruit farm-girls from this nation's wastelands: Nebraska, North Dakota, and northern Minnesota. Until they speak to each other and compare notes (and a wise suburbanite will do her best to keep her au pair incommunicado for as long as possible), girls from these states retain the refreshingly innocent idea that fifty dollars plus room and board is executive pay.

As in life, always seek balance when selecting an au pair. A Wonder Bread hog shuffling the supermarket aisles in crushed-heel slippers is disgusting, and reflects poorly on the household that set her loose in public. On the other hand, trim and attractive farmgirls will lose you your husband—just ask Mrs. Richard Dreyfuss. Always demand a photograph, preferably certified by the girl's pastor.

Foreign sources for au pairs are limited, but an enterprising employer may search in any of the Scandinavian countries, excepting Finland, which is suspiciously close to the potato-bloated Russians. Beware, European girls can convert dollars into their native currency with the aplomb of a euro-trader.

Unacceptable source countries include all of eastern Europe, France (self-explanatory), and Italy (hairy armpits, and likely to have dangerous relatives in the States). The English are off-limits until Louise Woodward finds the real killers.

Nannies are a separate category. These women don't change diapers and never, ever baby-sit at night. They must be Scottish and old enough to have raised the master of the suburban home when he was just a wee bairn. If the master's Brooklyn childhood has somehow become public knowledge, then it is acceptable for Nanny to have been the trusted servant of an Aunt Mary in Philadelphia, long ago. You must have one nanny for each child; anything less shouts "poor!"

## Other Household Help

Despite pleas from our children ("Mom, the next time we hire a maid, can we please get somebody who speaks English?"), domestic staff is best recruited from the Third World. You may have to make do with a hiring service when you first move into the suburbs, but as your club contacts grow, as you meet and are befriended by the moms at the day school, you will eventually be invited to join the "Filipino Connection" (in Texas and California, of course, it's the "Mexican Connection"; either way, it's the local pipeline to those hardworking, easily exploited little brown people without whom modern living would just be impossible). If you promise not to overpay her, you will be given the name of a particularly docile, matronly lady from our former colonial possession. Never break the code and slip the woman an extra dollar or two per day or she will talk, and your friends will find out and your access to this indispensable pipeline will be severed, forever. The ultimate faux pas is to lure away another's domestic by offering higher pay. Even if the woman whose household you raid is your deepest enemy, never succumb to temptation. Friendships in the suburbs can survive many personal betrayals, but when it comes to domestics and class solidarity, the woman who steals another's maid is playing with personal, permanent banishment. "Better to take my husband than my baby-sitter" is not a humorous observation in the suburbs.

# ENTERTAINING

Suburban nightlife is all about being seen—seen at the right places and with the right people. This essential element of a successful social life can be partially provided by dining out three times a week (twice in the suburbs, once in the city) at appropriate restaurants with appropriate people, but the real work is done at home: ours or others. You will want to host at least five gatherings a month, ranging from intimate dinner parties for twenty to full-bore social events, preferably involving fund-raising for a suitable charity.

Your cook can possibly manage the smaller dinner parties, but you'll never go wrong using the services of the caterer who

works for all your friends. Besides whipping up those tiny sand-
wiches we all adore, a good caterer can surprise and delight us
with any number of goodies. We're an adventurous bunch out
here and caterers know it, so be prepared for oysters and even
crayfish! Yummy with a capital *Y*!

You must host at least four special events each year: birthday
parties for you and your spouse, plus a spring and summer or fall
event. All of these require the services of an event designer, who will
ensure that your function will be the most talked about party of the
week. A whorehouse re-created in Bedford and disco dancing on a
Plexiglas dance floor installed over a Corona del Mar swimming
pool have already been done, as have drag queens and transvestite
dancers encased in Saran Wrap, but any event designer worth his
smelling salts can easily dream up something equally outlandish for
your special needs. You'll pay design fees of $15,000 to $75,000 and
expenses that bulldoze their way well into the six figures, but as one
event designer puts it, "Giving parties has become part of the image
packaging we're all trying to sell these days." What's *your* image? Do
you want it to be just another word for unimportant? You go, girl!

When dining out, the only rule one need remember is to
always send at least one item back as too coarse for your refined
palate. Some restaurants assume that just because they charge $275
for a bottle of wine and $75 for an entrée, the public will be too
intimidated to demand quality. Not you! There may well be nothing wrong with the wine; in fact, there probably isn't. That doesn't
mean you shouldn't sniff the cork, assume a sneering look of dis-
dain, and loudly demand a new bottle. You will awe your dining
companions (the restaurateur, having witnessed this spectacle every
night, will be less impressed) and, if your children are present, will
inculcate the same imperious air in them. If there is anything cuter

than seeing a budding six-year-old epicure reject his McDonald's Happy Meal because the fries are soggy, this writer hasn't seen it!

# HOLIDAYS

Holidays can be troublesome in the suburbs, for this is when relatives expect to visit. Those of you who don't want a fleet of battered Pontiacs descending, bearing parents, aunts, and uncles who will gawk at your new possessions and ask awkward questions about utility, may want to avoid the problem entirely by doing what so many of us do: flee. We like to reserve a family compound on St. Barts for the entire Christmas holiday, making sure that there are absolutely no spare bedrooms to accommodate Uncle Rebozo. This technique provides a plausible excuse for what might otherwise be considered rudeness, and spares us the embarrassment of explaining our heritage to our new friends in the community.

Thanksgiving can be dealt with the same way, providing you've purchased that Bar Harbor retreat, but sometimes there's simply no choice but to invite the swarm and be done with it. If this is the case, remember that darkness falls early in November, so set dinner for seven, with a mandatory minimum arrival time of five o'clock. There is simply no greater mortification than that which befalls the hostess who serves her turkey at noon, thereby unleashing a mob of elderly, disheveled relatives on the local streets for a postprandial daylight stroll.

Fleeing our relatives on holidays won't solve the problem of seasonal entertaining, of course, and this provides another occasion for event designers, who, with far more taste than us, will put together an entire evening that shows us to our best advantage.

When we suddenly remember that Christmas is a week away, for instance, only an experienced event designer can save us from disaster. He or she will select the proper Christmas tree, light it, and decorate it in a unique way. (The *New York Times* describes a stunning creation of a Mr. David Beahm's, who festoons his clients' trees with real—but dead, one imagines—blowfish and dried starfish draped in pearls. The trees must positively shriek "Merry Christmas!") Handing over decorating chores to an event

designer is a real time-saver for today's busy families; we spend so little time together, why squander it struggling with balky wiring when there are people who *do* that sort of thing? Expect to pay anywhere from $20,000 to $50,000 for decorations on each holiday. There is simply no price too high for the right statement, made to the right people. Besides that, you'll be creating memories your children will cherish forever.

Speaking of memories, those of us who live where snow does

not thrive can still provide our children with a white Christmas. For as little as $750 and as much as $10,000 landscaping companies will cover our acreage in artificial snow (the lower price yields only a faint whisper of winter, naturally). Imagine the effect upon your neighbors when they see snowdrifts towering over your stone walls and piled against your gated entrance while their own lawns are brown and bare. Who is God's chosen now?

# APPROPRIATE SUBURBAN-HOUSEWIFE WHINING

World hunger, philandering politicians, and the disintegration of Russia are, let's face it, pretty dull conversational fare, especially when our peer group doesn't read newspapers. Men talk of their new IPOs and dangerous option straddles and golf, but what can the suburban housewife do to show that she's not just a contented cow grazing on the largess of her warrior? She can complain, of course, and here's a list of guaranteed conversation starters:

- Husband spends all his time traveling on business; he's never home to help with the kids.
- Husband doesn't make enough money—if he didn't play golf on Sundays, he could put more time in at the office and you could afford that Chagal you saw last weekend on your Paris trip.
- It's almost an impossible burden to juggle the daily schedule when you have two tennis groups the same day as your personal training session *and* school pickup. How's a woman to cope?

- Your cell phone cut out in Topanga Canyon just when you were about to successfully conclude a play-date swap!
- The dust and inconvenience of your $3 million renovation project; the dollar amount—over a million dollars, naturally—is always mentioned when complaining about this one. As in, "You'd think for three point two million the damn contractor could provide a few dust barriers!"
- No valet parking at Kay Bee Toys!
- You can't find a reliable sub for your tennis group—it's ruining your life!
- Breaking in the new housekeeper.
- That cheap husband of yours gave you his old Palm Pilot III while he kept the new model. What's he got to keep track of, compared to you?
- Why do *you* have to do all the social planning? If it was up to him, your husband would come home Friday night and just collapse in the home theater.
- The Mercedes dealer actually tried to give you a Toyota Avalon as a loaner car!
- The stress of negotiating just the right table at the charity auction and the seating placement of your peers.

These are just suggestions. Remember to never show gratitude and always display a cynical displeasure with your world, and you'll be fine. One word of warning: while husbands are fair game and criticism of them will only enhance your status—it shows that you're aggressive and not willing to settle for anything but the best—our children are all perfect. If they aren't, it's a sign of bad genes, and you, my dear, are responsible for at least half of that problem. Mum's the word!

# PUBLICITY

## The Police Blotter

Life in the (proper) suburbs is blessedly free of serious crime. This advantage holds its downside: our local papers use the deeply personal events of our lives as filler to wrap around their advertisements. Run a stop sign, let your dog wander unleashed in the park, or fail to pay a few library fines and your peccadillo will be smeared across the front page faster than you can whisper "humiliation." Drunken-driving arrests or fights with spouses or girlfriends will be displayed prominently, and only the most well connected of our citizens can keep them from the paper. If you understand that the average suburban reporter is a twenty-five-year-old journalism school graduate earning less than your own child's weekly allowance, you will understand her deep, abiding resentment and her fervid desire to expose our flaws, and you will govern your conduct accordingly. You're being watched.

## Society News

There are, thankfully, other, more positive avenues of social recognition, principally in the society pages of the newspaper and the town's froufrou magazine: *Greenwich Magazine, Lake Forest Review, Westport,* and *Charleston Living* are all examples of such fare. These organs will publish just about anything you submit, so do so as often as possible. Your peers do read this stuff—it passes for literature in a crowd that once read *Portrait of the Artist as a Young Dog* in college and claimed to be Joyce scholars—and if they encounter your name often enough they will come to believe that you must be somebody important and start inviting you to their parties. Soon you *will* be important and can host your own soirees. One

**You must subscribe to your local Swells' magazine as well as appear in it. Otherwise, you'd miss exciting stories like this one:**

The steps of the Seventh Regiment Armory in Manhattan saw some wacky doings last week when Honey Brooks and her husband, Bob, broke their Nantucket fall vacation to attend the White Birch Polo Team's annual ball. As she entered the aging but still magnificent brick edifice, Honey almost bumped into the elderly grandmother of one of the grooms, wearing the same dress she was! A social disaster of the first order.

"I didn't come with a purse," Honey recounts, "so I said to Bob, 'Quick! Give me your credit card, I'm going shopping.' But he wouldn't. 'You're crazy,' he said. 'You look fine, and the Grand Procession starts in fifteen minutes.'

" 'Well, I'm not going to be seen anywhere in this city without a new dress,' I told him. Nothing could have stopped me. I just *would not* be embarrassed."

Then up into the saddle swung fellow attendee John Gilbert. "Hey," cried he, flashing his American Express card, "there are a million stores in this city—Hi, Ho Platinum and away!"

Honey and John raced across the street to a charming boutique Honey had noticed coming in, and Honey snapped at the first saleswoman she saw. "Look. I have no time, and I *have* to have a dress. Bring me anything, *anything* in size six.

"And," Honey adds, "they brought me a little black suit, your basic Prada." At Honey's command, the staff also brought in a pearl ensemble: necklace, bracelet, and earrings, and a little velvet bag for her diamonds, which couldn't *possibly* go with her new outfit. John gave them his card and signed a blank charge form without ever learning the price.

"I didn't care what it cost," Honey giggles. "This was an emergency." The couple sprinted back across Seventh Avenue just in time to join the Grand Procession.

"I'll always cherish John for riding to my rescue," Honey sighs, "but I've forgiven Bob. He would have done the right thing had he only understood; he just thought I was being silly."

tip to hasten this process: always use address hyphenation in your press releases, as in "Mr. and Mrs. Corwood Jones III of La Jolla–Catalina" or "Egbert Pennington, Greenwich-Nantucket" will do nicely, even if the closest you've ever been to an island is a rented beach bungalow on Cape Cod.

## MUNICIPAL SERVICES

Although we prefer to think that both death and taxes are evadable (that's what seven-grain wheat bread and high colonics are all about), we of this new age demand a full offering of every imaginable town service, and if everyone's property taxes must quadruple to provide them, well, that's just the way it must be; we'll make it up by evading the federal predators. Our parks will be spotless (even if we use them only as drive-by scenery), our roads and (separate) bicycle lanes pampered and lovingly paved, and there will be five police officers for every hundred citizens, damn the expense! If there's a town library, it will be useful:

dozens of computer terminals linked via cable modem to the Internet, extensive business research material, a Starbucks café, and a children's reading room fully staffed with trained child-care providers so that moms can drop off their toddlers while they themselves continue on to a guilt-free exercise class.

Every rotary at every intersection will be manicured and beflowered, litter will not exist, and our town selectman or mayor will be someone selected from our own ranks, rather than a professional, so we can chat him up at the golf club. Our concerns are his concerns, and if they aren't, we make them so. All this costs money, but so what? We didn't work this hard to accumulate this much money just so we could be ignored, did we?

Dear Whitney:

My husband's fortieth birthday is fast approaching, and I want to throw him a party that he (and all of our friends!) will be talking about for weeks! Can you suggest something that will knock 'im out of his cowboy boots?

Cowgirl from Evergreen, Colorado

# From the Desk of Whitney

Dear Cowgirl in the Sand:

You bet I can! First, make it a party de ranchero: everyone, and that includes the catering crew, must come in their prettiest, most colorful western garb (the caterers should wear blue ultrasuede sashes to avoid embarrassing confusion—if you've ever spent ten minutes chatting up a fellow guest only to discover that he's actually in charge of serving the coleslaw, you'll know what I mean). The guests, limited to an intimate size—250 or so—should arrive just before sunset and be greeted by elegant, white-tableclothed rounds set about the pool, each sporting a lovely and unique flower arrangement (budget $1,000 per table to ensure proper quality, plus $10,000 to $15,000 for a formal centerpiece). Leave selection of the proper hors d'oeuvres to the caterer—she'll know what to do, but insist upon spitted steers for the main course. Nothing is more impressive than four or five full-sized cow carcasses roasting over an ocean of coals. After dessert and a warm-up round of square dancing, bring out the best, bring out Willie! Mr. Nelson is currently available for house calls ($100,000 plus expenses, but keep your eye on the newspapers—if the IRS continues to plague the poor man, you may be able to grab his services for far less). If all this isn't enough to boost you (temporarily—after all, you'll have raised the bar, and who doesn't love a challenge?) to the top of the Colorado social whirl, you can (a) move to Alabama or (b) hire the Beatles. Bon soirée!

# Chapter 6

# CLOTHING

# MEN'S CLOTHING

**Casual**

On or near the water, the well-dressed suburban male will still favor the traditional combination of (handmade) blazer, Breton reds, and Top-Siders. It's the last little vestige of Prep in our changed world, and provides a refreshing sense of continuity to our life in the fast lane. We envied the Preps when they were on top; now we can afford to adopt a few of their quaint customs as an ironic tribute to their passing; imagine yourself as a conquering Roman, daubing on blue Celtic body paint and you'll get the picture. Your Top-Siders, by the way, will be new: the only people wearing old shoes these days are those too poor to buy a new pair, and that's not your problem or you wouldn't be reading this book.

Golfing wear is permissively louder, though natural fibers should be selected whenever possible (some pant patterns simply cannot be extracted from nature's bounty). Around town, freshly pressed corduroy trousers and penny loafers (polished, please!) are always acceptable, so long as the blue blazer—don't leave the docks without it—is slung over a shoulder. Shirts are button-down Oxfords or a collared tee, preferably with a high-tech-company or hedge-fund logo on the breast. Wild socks are considered by investment bankers to show a devil-may-care recklessness and can be experienced at "fun" formal events.

Shooting clothes have grown in acceptance, now that the game of sporting clays has separated guns from bird blood. Take a look at the gentleman depicted here for an example of how this look is assembled. Custus Turbot is wearing a two-and-a-quarter-inch-brimmed loden hat and a tweed stockton barn jacket. The leather piping on his pocket edges shows that Cus has eschewed the until now obligatory suede elbow patches and elected instead to make a subtle, ironic reference to the past. He's donned cavalry tweed trousers (cuffed, of course), and that's a Beretta over-and-under he's carrying. The gloves are pigskin, the tie shows his status as

a former governor at his yacht club, and the shooter's bag by his foot is by Gucci. What a package, what a guy!

The Old Preps rejected marketers like Ralph Lauren out of a Yankee sense of thrift—why pay $600 extra for a fuzzy polo player on the pocket? When Mr. Lifshitz made his wares available to the shoppers of Sam's Club and Costco, his fate should have been sealed, for no one in their right mind would wear the same clothes as his gardener, would they? But in our New Suburbia we can bask in the security of knowing our gardener will never appear at the same public functions we do. So spend away—anything Ralph sells will be entirely acceptable and appropriately priced, at the stores where we shop.

## At the Office

Custom suits only on Monday through Thursday. Casual Fridays are the perfect time to experiment with merino wool slacks and a tieless shirt, but be especially careful on dress-up days. An off-the-rack or made-to-measure Paul Stuart may have served the old guard well enough, but the men who wore them bought them at Yale, kept them through their careers, and ended by being buried in them. You don't want that to happen to you, so dump your old clothes at the thrift shop for bums to wear and drop the $7,000 to $10,000 per issue for a custom wardrobe that speaks of and to you alone. An inside lining made from cut-up Hermès ties is optional, but a ticket pocket on the breast and functioning button-holes on the sleeves are not; you'll want to leave the latter undone when power lunching. The eminent, if rather short, custom-suited economist Lawrence Kudlow tells the *New York Times,* "The more prosperous the man, the more difficult it is to satisfy his needs," and doesn't that just say it all? Do *you* want to be seen as someone easily satisfied? Shirts, shoes, and ties must, of course, also be handmade to your exact fit or the suit's effect will be ruined.

## Formal

*"The severest mortification a gentleman can incur*
*is to attract observation in the street by*
*his outward appearance."*

—BEAU BRUMMEL

In modern English, this simply means that one's formal wear must be boring. No bottle-green or red cummerbunds, please, and while bow ties on strings or metal clips may suffice for a poorly trained staff, they will never do for the properly dressed suburbanite, Prep or newcomer. Thank you.

# WOMEN'S CLOTHING

## Casual

There is no such thing. Even spandex-encased, personal-trainer-shaped thighs must always be topped by cashmere and pearls.

## Formal

The properly dressed woman will be five foot ten, one hundred and five pounds, and dressed in black pants. Her cell phone (in a coordinated color, of course) may be stashed in her Kate Spade bag or a Prada—her choice, but remember that Kate Spade is considered the poor woman's Prada and choose accordingly.

A beeper, carried at all times in case there is a change in the child's play-date schedule, is worn on the belt or stored in that same bag. The only other required accessory is her diamond, no smaller than six carats. This latter item is worn constantly to all events, formal or informal, and especially at the health club.

## Shoes

Prada, Gucci, or anything from Jeffrey (Fourteenth Street in New York). One fun choice at Jeffrey is a pair of Manolo Blahnik pink high-heeled mules with rhinestone clips–$875 the pair, and you wouldn't want to actually walk in them, but then again, we're talking fashion here; if you want to be mistaken for an aging, out-of-style Prep, call L. L. Bean.

## Accessories

Hermès forever. And lots of tiny, expensive watches. One new fashion trend not to be missed is shahtoosh, the fine, delicate wool obtained from the carcass of the Tibetan antelope. Outwardly similar to the far more common pashmina, a shahtoosh, or "ring shawl," costs at least $4,950, and that's all you and your friends need to know. You will want a collection of shahtooshes in a rainbow of colors, as well as undergarments, sweaters, blankets ($20,000 and up), and whatever else you can lay your hands on. And the laying is growing increasingly more difficult: the Tibetan antelope is endangered, and, unlike more plebeian goats, can't be shorn while alive. A bunch of spoilsports from the U.S. Customs Service has been subpoenaing shahtoosh owners, demanding that they turn over their illicit garments and pay hefty fines. Pat Buckley swears that she's never heard of "anything so ridiculous" and Christie Brinkley vows that they'll have to pry her shahtooshes from her "cold, stiff fingers," but remember when we could wear our leopardskin coats on Fifth Avenue? Stock up now.

# CHILDREN'S CLOTHING

Clothes for our infants are traditional (smocking, smocking, smocking), then Abercrombie & Fitch, Tommy Hilfiger, and Victoria's Secret for older girls—six years and up. For infants, Monica Noel and La Chatelaine have wonderful lines, with collars embroidered with sweet peas and strawberries. Very chic. Ditto for Papo d'Anjo, who holds trunk shows in all our best cities and suburbs. If you have more than one child, it's always cute to do matching, and lederhosen for small boys is adorable.

Boys are a bit of a problem to dress, particularly when father interferes. Papo has now redesigned its U.S. line to include squared collars for boys, mainly to appease our husbands, who

object to round little Dutch-boy collars as effeminate; they know nothing, but Papo d'Anjo knows who pays the bills.

Anthea Moore Ede, of London, takes orders for made-to-measure outfits, which may be a problem if your child grows like Topsy, but then, is it ever too soon to start our girls on the water-biscuit-and-Perrier diet? Hermès makes adorable baby blankets and quilted jackets, handmade underwear is readily available in all the better shops, and Versace, Moschino, Dries Van Noten, and Dior all do children's. Barneys carries mini Missoni. All appropriate, and don't forget TSE's fabulous cashmere sweaters!

Also don't forget floppy hair bows. Here in the suburbs, they're known as "player bows," referring to the parents—the bigger the bow, the bigger the player. Some of the girls belonging to the biggest players walk around like lop-eared rabbits, but can any price be too large for a parent's prestige?

# Chapter 7

# THE PERFECT CHILD

> *"I don't spoil my children—I just give them*
> *anything they want."*
>
> —NEEDLEPOINT PILLOW OFFERED BY SINCERELY YOURS,
> YOUR GUIDE FOR ELEGANT LIVING ($275)

We moved to the suburbs for our children's benefit, and life here revolves around the precious darlings. They are perfect, and we will protect and shape them to ensure that they stay that way. Here are some of the ways we do so.

# A GOOD START

You will certainly have your first child while still in the city; sophisticates don't abandon the fun, fast urban life for the desolation of seventeen acres of manicured lawn until the presence of a swarming brood forces them to acquire more space than is available in almost any apartment. Your child will be perfect, of course, but to ensure this you will want to select the very finest obstetrician in the city. Ask your friends (call them in the suburbs, if need be), and you'll be directed to just the right doctor. You'll want one who will induce you in an emergency—a big party, for instance—and not one of the new, back-to-nature, alternative types who won't give you drugs during delivery. In New York, the East Side houses these accommodating types, and they'll be affiliated with New York Hospital or Columbia. Avoid the West Side and its "birthing centers," God forbid; you'll get tofu instead of epidurals, and, honey, they ain't the same. In other areas of our country, rely on other mothers for advice, but stay away from moms who prefer Birkenstocks and ankle-length skirts to 9 West and CK, and you will be directed to exactly the right sort of place.

# SAFETY

Before that precious bundle even arrives home, you will want to have transformed your house into a "child-safe" environment. No risk is acceptable here; none at all. Just as, later, in the suburbs, your child will be wearing safety helmets for riding his Big Wheel on the driveway, skiing, and playing on swings (although these latter dangerous instruments have been almost completely eliminated from playgrounds by the concerned parents who have gone before you), the city apartment will offer no hidden hazards to the careful mom. The crib (the bars of which will be covered in solid plywood so that Precious doesn't get a finger stuck) will have head, foot, and side bumpers, thereby forcing the little one to lie on her side. Any other position—on her back (1980s advice) or on her stomach (1970s)—might cause a warped skull plate, with a concomitant exclusion from the better nursery schools. The proper position for 2001 has yet to be announced, but when it is, you can be sure that all the better baby stores will have exactly the right bumpers, helmets, ropes, or hand restraints necessary for conforming your care to the new standard of vigilance.

City or suburb, every cabinet must be locked, every electrical outlet plugged, and every toilet-bowl lid securely bolted down. Buckets (danger of drowning!) are banned from the house until our youngest is at least twelve years old, and none of us will ever engage in any sport without the proper safety equipment, so that we can demonstrate proper caution to our children. This means knee and wrist guards for roller blading; safety goggles and appropriately padded, Lycra spandex bumblebee shorts for bicycle riding; always strapping in, even when moving the

Beemer from one end of the driveway to the other; and always, *always!* wearing a Bell-certified safety helmet for every outside activity.

# BABY'S LIVING SPACE
# IN THE CITY

You will want a separate apartment for baby and nanny to share. "If you get the child their own apartment, it should at least be connecting," reports *Vogue,* and that's advice worth considering, even if such an arrangement raises the noise level to inappropriate levels during dinner parties. The infant's room will be profession-ally decorated, and, again, *Vogue* has a wise word here: "I'm sus-picious," the magazine quotes one young East Sider as saying, "of the children's industry. This primary-color crap. So what if it's good for the baby's development? It's hideous." Indeed it is. Listen to your decorator and relax.

# BABY'S LIVING SPACE
# IN SUBURBIA

This is one of the reasons you moved from the city in the first place: space. Baby and nanny will be quartered in the ten-thousand-square-foot children's wing, far removed from the serene adult world. Comments on decorating city apartments apply with equal force here, but the sky's the limit. There's no need to waste resources on the nanny—a Scottish privy and a single cot will do nicely—but baby will need a mini–master bath, plus Thomas Moser handcrafted cherry bunk beds, chairs, tables, and toy chests. A big-screen television for *Sesame Street* and chil-dren's videos, a music entertainment center that blasts Raffi and "Baby Beluga" off the rafters, and a hand-painted wall mural depicting cheery farm animals will all contribute to baby's envi-ronment. Since you will want the child reading at a sixth-grade level before preschool, this wing is the place for books; the local bookstore in your town (have your staff check the Yellow Pages) will send over cartons of material, and the nanny will take charge from there.

# SCHOOLS

Aside from your fellow club members, your social circle in suburbia will be restricted to the parents of your children's schoolmates—in fact, your club and your child's school directory are the only phone lists you will ever need, so choose that school carefully. Preschool should be (Protestant) church sponsored, regardless of one's own attendance at any such institution. Public grammar schools, kindergarten through fifth grade, are acceptable, provided they are located in the proper areas of your town. You won't, however, know which is which until you move to the suburbs, so play it safe: *never* leave the city until your children have been accepted into a private academy.

Middle school and high school choices are restricted to traditional private day or boarding institutions—public education at this level simply means that you're poor. Montessori schools or any of those "Let's spend fifteen weeks on Vermont's Long Trail" may be fine for the Old Money set with nothing left to lose, but not for us. Stick to the tried and true, which means institutions requiring uniforms consisting of sport coats and ties for the young gentlemen and plaid skirts or jumpers and white blouses for the ladies. No hikes during the academic year (Outward Bound is an essential hardening experience for every child, but it may be attended during the summer) and no soft, fuzzy teachers for *our* children—we're in this game to win, and if our children don't like it, why, they can just go and find another family to live with!

College: In Old Suburbia, one merely notified one's alma mater of the birth of a male child and, just before the end of his senior year, sent a quiet reminder note that Orthwaith would be arriving the next fall. Assuming the necessary bequests had been

It is possible, of course, that a new science wing will be a bit beyond your reach in the early days of your career. Just to make sure that your child gets into the college of your choice, here are the extracurricular activities that will guarantee success: working with the handicapped (especially the retarded, for some reason); varsity sports (by their sophomore year, or don't bother); Operation Safe Rides volunteer; orchestra, including a performance at Carnegie Hall (relax—they rent the place out by the evening); a purported interest in opera (shows the child isn't homophobic); founding member, Student Gay-Straight Alliance (same as the preceding—plus, if carefully worded, it leaves admissions guessing as to child's orientation, and they can count him twice for quota purposes); thespian activities; and being a member of any number of made-up groups: the "Cleisophics Society" or "Students Against Hunger" are just two examples.

Bear in mind that mere participation in all of these organizations is not enough: your child must be the president of every service organization, star of every play and musical, and founder of whatever fictional organizations your family (and college applications are very much a combined effort) dreams up. If there is any danger that the real president of, say, Operation Safe Rides will apply to the same school, claim a "co-presidency." Your child will look refreshingly modest, while the real McCoy will be revealed as a credit-hogging braggart.

attended to at the passing of various ancestors, admission was a certainty. This has changed.

Many of us out here in the 'burbs didn't quite make it to the Ivies—a few too many whiffs from the old bong, perhaps, but there is no reason why our children, perfect as they are, should not go where we could not. We all want our children to matriculate on hallowed grounds, but if our own fathers never graduated from the state agricultural college, let alone bequeathed a few odd million to Harvard, how can we get them there? Fortunately, these fine old institutions still respond to the scent of lucre, and that's the one thing we have a lot of. Assuming Gramps doesn't have a few campus buildings honoring him already, you've got eighteen years to make up for lost time. That's enough, so long as you start immediately. Contribute to the Ivy of your choice as soon as your firstborn arrives, and keep it up every year, never quitting until the last of your brood is admitted. Host fund-raisers for the school at your home, being sure to be identified as the largest benefactor. Snoop around; is there some painting that the school's art director considers a "must have"? Buy it for the fellow! A new science wing needed? Build it! The best-coached SAT taker doesn't stand a chance against the son of the man who endowed three chairs, so get out your checkbook and keep it out until you've wrung an acceptance from the dean of admissions. We'd remind you never to take no as an answer, but if you're one of us, you already know that.

# SPORTS

*"That's all right, that's okay,
you'll all work for us someday."*

—PRIVATE SCHOOL CHANT SUNG BY PARENTS AND STUDENTS
TOGETHER WHEN LOSING TO A PUBLIC SCHOOL'S TEAM

Just as our children no longer engage in informal pickup baseball or soccer games after school, suburban parents never, ever interfere with their child's athletic development by "playing catch." We hire sports tutors for our children, and we wouldn't dare jeopardize that learning process with a careless toss of a lacrosse ball. Children's sports are, for parents, strictly a spectator activity (although correcting the coach's tactics from the sidelines is expected and desirable, as it shows a seemly parental concern for the welfare of our beloved athletic star). Both parents are expected to attend each and every "away" game; the only excuses acceptable for this breach of duty are that a missing parent is attending another child's away game in another town or, for dads only, a business trip. While suburban life's orbit does indeed center on our children, there is another, superior galaxy that overrides all other considerations: the world of business. Fathers may travel to this world at any time, with no loss of social esteem.

Acceptable sports include soccer, squash, tennis, field hockey for the girls, ski teams, and golf. While football and ice hockey were always indulged in by the Preps, they've acquired a new popularity under our generation because these are, now, truly "hardball." Flying elbows, sticks, and fists make little warriors out of our otherwise pampered children and, by God, that's what it takes to survive and triumph in this world. All of the listed sports have summer camps entirely devoted to perfection of the appropriate skills. By combining private lessons during the school year and ten-week camp sessions, we can ensure that our children succeed where others fail, and isn't that fun!

# UNSCHEDULED TIME

There is no such thing in our lives. Every minute of ours must be planned, and every second of our children's. For under tens,

Preps used Day-Timers to schedule their time, and so did their children, who were each presented one on their eighth birthday. The remaining Preps, many of whom have hung on to important positions in our charitable organizations, still use these quaint devices as status signals, so you will want to be able to read the code and decide which old lady to make nice to. As a rule, size is dictated by responsibilities. If the Prep's a really big real estate broker or head of a really big committee, then she'll have a really big Day-Timer. Small duties, smaller planner. Don't be fooled by those silly Preps who attempt to overstate their importance by flaunting planners too large for their position. Check with your friends; if the lady's a pretender, you may treat her with the scorn she so obviously deserves.

What went into a Day-Timer? Only everything, darling, just like your own Palm Pilot IV: numbers for all the essential service providers (the hair stylist and masseuse), every play date, every personal-trainer appointment, every committee meeting, luncheon with the girls, and so forth and so on. In the unlikely event that a Prep discovered an empty time slot, she'd fill it in immediately with *something!* God forbid, a snoopy snoop might learn that she wasn't "maxed out," and if her time wasn't completely prescheduled, then she must be unimportant and friendless. Ugh!

this schedule will be: homework, school, after-school play dates, homework, dinner, and quality time with Mom. Once they've reached fifth grade, the kids will expect their own credit card and the use of a driver so that they can date without fear of being dependent on a parent. Weekends will be devoted to travel-team sports, which require their own subchapter, as follows.

# TRAVEL TEAMS

Our children do not engage in pickup games of baseball, or compete in townwide sports leagues open to all. No, we entrust our children to the travel teams—highly selective and very expensive, as all good things are. Parents new to the suburbs often come a cropper here because sometimes, especially when a coach has not yet learned who you are, he may place your budding Olympian on the B or C team or even (yes, it can happen, even in the safest suburbs) deny him admission at all! You must not let this happen. Not only will your child's exuberant spirit be crushed, probably permanently, but you, as parents, will miss out on the primary weekend daytime social activity, attending A-team travel games. This is what you bought the Ford Excursion for, after all, and this is why caterers open early on Saturdays to serve you. Attendance at your child's games shows that you are a concerned parent, it demonstrates that, no matter how much you make at work (and your choice of clothes and vehicle will make it quite clear that you make a lot), you still have your priorities straight; and, most important, it gives you the opportunity to mingle with the best parents in town. By definition, a B-team player comes from inferior stock, so unless you want to rub shoulders with the grease-stained shoulders of the local attorney or dentist, you and your child will make certain to be A-team players. And how will you ensure that? You will yell. You will be courteous to the A-team coach before player selection begins, but if he double-crosses you, if he fails to properly investigate and learn exactly who you are and what your position is in town society, you will react accordingly. Angry calls at his workplace and residence, at all hours of the day, should do the trick nicely, and quickly. If escalation is

est. 1888
BROOKHAVEN
SPORTS CAMP
FOR
YOUNG LADIES
LACROSSE CAMP
EQUESTRIAN CAMP
SQUASH CAMP
FIELD HOCKEY CAMP
TENNIS CAMP

demanded, go for his wife, child, dog, or whoever else happens to pick up the phone. Very soon, the gentleman will remember that he is a volunteer, and decide that he isn't getting paid enough to take the steady stream of invective flowing from the receiver. He will capitulate.

Travel teams have specific seasons, but training never stops. Your children will require private tutors or coaches if they are to excel, at the game and in life, so Mom or the family driver must take them to the best instructors in the area. Often, this involves three trips a week to the city for private lessons, but when it comes to our children, is any inconvenience too great? You will soon see why we insist that our au pairs and nannies all hold valid driving licenses, and why five-car garages are not considered excessive in the proper suburban home.

Don't despair! Relief from the onerous duty of supervising all this activity arrives each summer, when we ship the children off to (the best, naturally) sleep-away camps for further training. These exist for all the basic food groups: tennis, squash, and lacrosse, and for the young ladies, hockey and equestrian sports. That takes care of the period from mid-May through end of July, leaving only August, when, of course, the little athletes will rejoin the family in Nantucket.

# CHRISTMAS LETTERS

How will our friends know of our children's prowess if we don't tell them? The composition of the family Christmas letter can be assigned to Mom or Dad, but whoever writes it must be sure to include glowing mention of the following areas:

Grades: honor roll or higher (and if we're fudging a bit here, we make certain to mail this letter only to out-of-town friends whose children don't attend school with ours);

Admissions and graduations, from nursery to graduate school;

Team captainships (see cautionary note on grades, above);

Cute witticisms;

Vacation travels of each child and their easy mastery of new people skills;

Celebrities the children encountered and quotes from those people attesting to your offspring's adult-like sophistication ("Henry turned to us and said, in that gorgeous German accent, 'I have not met a lady mit your daughter's grasp of global politics since I vorked mit Prime Minister Thatcher.' Just wait, Dr. K, until Libby's nine!").

The more modest among us may feel a slight tremor of apprehension over displaying the extraordinary accomplishments of our children to our friends, but remember: they'll be sending you news of their own children, and unless you reciprocate, you know who wins that bit of Yuletide sharing.

Dear Whitney:

I'm just worried to death about young Trevor. His pre-PSATs are dreadful, his grades are worse, and he mopes around the house all day smoking pot. I suspect he's worried about his diminutive size, as his father, Henry, bless the man, is only five foot four and Trevor hasn't budged five feet. Should I give him growth hormones now, or wait until he's in fifth grade?

(The third) Ms. K, NYC

# From the Desk of Whitney

Dear Kay:

A few shots of HGH certainly can't hurt, so go for it, but here's another approach you won't want to overlook: have Trevor declared "learning disabled." Psychologists will diagnose the condition in anyone, and your boy will be furnished with private tutors, will receive special assistance (all at his school's expense) and, most important, will be permitted to take untimed P and SATs. What an advantage the lad will have over his unwashed competitors! Of course, he'll have plenty of (the right sort of) company while he takes those untimed tests, because the rest of us have also stumbled onto this marvelous idea; in Greenwich, one third of all high school students (and 85 percent of all students whose parents earn $250,000 or more) are "learning disabled." It's a benefit that flows to the wealthy and knowledge-able, and isn't that the way things *should* be?

# Chapter 8

# CARE OF THE SOUL

# ENTITLEMENT

Most of us, sadly, were not "to the manner born," and this occasionally causes conflicts when we encounter the last remaining holdouts of Old Money. They sneer at us, call us "nouveau riche" as though that were some kind of fault, and play games with our self-esteem when we apply to their private clubs. Well, by gosh, our money's as good as theirs, and we have more of it! How do we put these relics, these doddering old snoots in their proper place? By acting, always, with the certain knowledge that we are an entitled class. Everything we have was well earned; everything we want—and we want it now—is deserved. "No, you can't do that," "No, you can't be admitted to this club," and "No, your child cannot be admitted to this school" (or travel team, etc.) are phrases we have never heard and that we do not recognize when they refer to our needs. Yes, we're entitled, and the little people damn well better get out of our way.

# DO YOU KNOW WHO I AM?

For all the complaining that salesclerks raise over our always asking this question, the sad truth is that they usually don't have a clue. Especially when summering, but even occasionally in your hometown, you must expect to encounter ignorant locals who lack any idea of the important position you hold as the spouse of an investment banker or the founder of one of this country's hottest high-tech operations. This can be maddening, and when, after throwing a memorable tantrum to leave a lasting impression, you visit the same shop a second time to see the effect and discover that the lazy fellow has made absolutely no attempt to learn who you are, well . . . a little justifiable rage is certainly in order. But don't give up; never accept such slothfulness as an excuse for anyone, anywhere, to treat you with indifference or disrespect, or you soon will be their equal, and that, my dear, means you'll have landed right back where you started from.

# MANNERS

We don't use them. Consideration of others is an admission that there are in fact "others" in our universe and is, therefore, never practiced among our set. Salesclerks exist to serve us, and may be treated accordingly. Drivers and pedestrians are merely obstacles to our own plans and may be honked at, blocked in, or cut off as our pleasure and needs dictate. This sounds a bit harsh, but readers who might otherwise quail at acting rudely need merely spend fifteen minutes in their local gourmet food store's parking lot witnessing the maneuvers of their neighbors, fresh from aerobics classes. These spandex terrors will quickly inspire the most horrid, self-defensive behavior in even the gentlest of souls.

Remember, whatever we want is ours, whether it is a parking space on Greenwich Avenue (and the delightful mayhem occasioned by a three-ton Lincoln Navigator swerving to the other lane to grab a space from a patiently waiting lesser creature is reason enough to indulge in this bit of aggressiveness) or admission to prep schools, restaurants, or life itself. Got a video to drop off and

can't find a parking space? You'll only be a few minutes, so park where you wish and don't worry about blocking other drivers. You may not be a master of the universe, but you certainly are its center, so do as you please and hang the rest. Lines, as they say, are for the little people, and you don't want to be perceived as one of them, ever.

That we inculcate this sense of entitlement in our children, however unconsciously, can be seen at any roadway abutting a private school. Watch the little darlings as they stride purposefully across, looking neither left nor right, secure in the certain knowledge that their need to cross when they want to will cause the rest of the world to pause. They're on their way!

# RELIGION

Life in suburbia is neither contemplative nor spiritual, so choose your church by the same criterion you use to select your family's transportation fleet. Flash on top of solidity is best, and you will generally find this felicitous combination among the Episcopalians. Congregationalists and Presbyterians can be boring, carrying just a tint of midwestern piety about them that will undermine your statement of social triumph. Avoid quirky sects like the Lutherans, the Baptists, and the RCs.

Regardless of the sects you consider, your primary question should be, How soon can I join the governing board? Attainment of a seat on the vestry or session confers instant status, and you will want to make certain that these coveted positions are not all locked in by the old guard. Again, suitably large-sized contributions will go a long way toward accelerating your rise to the top. Don't forget: membership at the right church also ensures admission for your children to its preschool, so don't go to just any church; you won't want to waste your Sunday morning at an institution whose preschool is not at the top of that particular ladder. Planning and foresight are essential

EVERYONE WILL BE THERE
**SWISS**
SPIRITUAL RETREAT
GOD + the ALPS
6 DAYS · 5 NIGHTS

in this regard, so don't be swayed by the first pretty steeple you discover.

Some readers may cringe at the thought of church—too many painful memories of scolding old clerics berating the parish for its callous treatment of the poor, its refusal to sponsor a soup kitchen, or the shabby treatment of domestics. Not to worry: there are churches just for us, and you'll find them by scouting the parking lots on Sunday morning. Nothing less prestigious than a Jaguar? Lots of Audi 8s and Range Rovers? You've arrived. Inside you'll find a soothing minister in custom-made shahtoosh vestments and an Ivy League ring (if male; a fifteen-carat diamond if female) cooing about Christ's special love for his favorite people. No stern lectures here on sharing what we've worked so hard to amass, and not even a whiff of industrial-sized cans of soup being heated in the kitchen for distribution to the poor. Tea and crumpets (just for us!) are served afterward as we cluster round the sign-up table for spiritual retreats to Switzerland. Be assured: relief missions to Guatemala are very much *not* included in our itinerary.

## SPIRITUALITY

Just kidding.

## ANGLOPHILISM

The new (and the old, come to think of it) suburbs worship and grovel in orgasmic debasement before anything and everything English. As we can't distinguish between the coarsest Cockney accent and the most stiff-lipped Etonian, your opportunities to impress your peers are unlimited. Bring home a news vendor, take him to dinner at your club, and introduce him around as Lord Falfax; your prestige will soar. Similarly, you will never go wrong bringing up in conversation the latest British import from the BBC, even *Benny Hill*. Furniture, clothing, books, and wallpaper—all will be fine so long as they're English.

# Chapter 9

# RECREATION

# CLUBS

As a proper suburbanite, you will prefer playing squash at the Field Club to handball at the Y. Relaxing on a yacht club's green lawn, toasting the sunset with a gin and tonic in the company of Cameron, Gideon, and William, is far, far better than towing your bass boat down a municipal ramp attended by Rick and Joe. There are a lot of ways to spend our weekends in the suburbs, but all the good ones involve clubs: country, yacht, tennis, polo, and sporting clays. In the proper town, all of these activities can be engaged in at municipal facilities, but if they're open to all, if anyone can get in, why would we want to join them? No, for us, the new suburbanite, private clubs are the proper venue for our entire recreational schedule, and that raises a problem: how does one gain admission to these sacred, exclusive grounds?

You must first understand that a club's primary mission is to serve as a buffer against the boors of the world (defined as anyone who isn't already a member), so merely expressing an interest in the particular activity that the club sponsors will get you nowhere. And please, don't pull up to the yacht-club marina in your Donzi and ask the launch boy for an admissions application: one particularly insecure commodore of a prestigious California yacht club was known to start every board meeting with yet another tale of a naive couple attempting just that, and it never failed to amuse his fellow officers.

Admission to clubs is by invitation only, but it's up to you to elicit that invitation. You'll need a sponsor, a Big Name (at the club, anyway), who does nothing other than splash his signature on the bottom of your application, and a co-sponsor, who is responsible for rounding up the necessary half dozen letters of recommendation from other members. When you've just moved in, this requirement can seem an insurmountable obstacle: you know exactly two people in the suburbs, and one is your garbageman. Like all of life's problems, however, this can be hurdled with relative ease.

Begin with the other person you know: your real estate agent. The best agents, and you did choose the best, are those who have clout at their clubs. While few agents will be so crass as to guarantee admission if you'll buy one of their listings, that's the unspoken quid quo pro. The right agent will become your new best friend in the community; she'll find a title head sponsor, enlist her husband to act as co-sponsor, and host the cocktail party where you're going to meet the writers of those letters of recommendation. When all that's accomplished, you will be invited to the admissions cocktail party. This soiree used to be merely a rubber-stamp process of approval, but that was when everyone at the club knew who your parents were. The flood of strangers into our better towns has transformed what was once a convivial catching up on the doings of the clan to a meticulous and searching inventory of our personality and background. Generally, it takes about five minutes.

To illustrate, lets look at two couples competing for the one available admissions slot. There's Tim and Edna, thirty-six and thirty-three years old, with two toddlers who both attend Kinder Kare™ nursery school; they live in a modest house in a good section of town. Tim's an architect with a New York City firm, and Edna is executive editor of a fashion magazine.

George and Hildy are the same ages as Tim and Edna and, in fact, live right down the street from them. They, too, have small children, but they're enrolled at Christ the Episcopal School of Grace, and Hildy has elected to stay at home instead of working. George is a vice president with Microbiotech.com.

Tim and Edna have sailed since they were children. Edna sailed only small boats, as she was raised in modest circumstances, but she knows the pointy end from the fat one. Tim worked as ship delivery captain after college and has sailed in five of the seven seas. George and Hildy have taken several captained charters in the Caribbean, and "just love" sailing.

The admissions committee has already decided in favor of George and Hildy before the meeting: bankers are less flighty than architects, as shown by the choice of School of Grace instead of the commercial Kinder Kare™, and stay-at-home Hildy will be available to serve on the house decoration and entertainment committees. Still, there have been some rumblings lately over the lack of sailing ability of the new members, so the committee

If, reading this, you realize that you've blundered by choosing the wrong school, picking the wrong neighborhood, or, God forbid, using a realtor without a club affiliation, don't despair—not, that is, if you live near a suitable body of water. You've lost your chance for admission to a golf or field club, but sailing may provide a way out of permanent social banishment. While yacht clubs are ordinarily as difficult to get into as any other institution, a hidden way exists, one based on the hard truth that old sailboats neither die nor fade away; fiberglass is forever. The owner of an old Pearson 36, circa 1973, or, worse, a New York 40 is stuck with it for life unless he finds a buyer, and that's where you come in, literally. In exchange for letting him unload his leaking, obsolete racer on you, this member will get you into his club. The admissions committee will look the other way (poor ol' Hopkins will never dump the thing otherwise), and there you'll be, with your own slip and your own bright new admissions certificate. Of course, you will also be faced with the problem of what to do with the aged glob of fiberglass, but another membership slot will open up eventually, eh?

has decided to take a look at Tim and Edna. The contest is over before Tim can finish his beer (George ordered white wine; Hildy, Perrier). Why? It is as clear as the bolo around Tim's neck.

Tim's been designing an art museum in Santa Fe, and he arrived late this afternoon from that city, still wearing his silver and turquoise bolo tie and cowboy boots. Edna had begged against it, but he'd decided to attend the meeting as is—after all, it's a sailing club they're joining, and doesn't his demonstrated interest in sailing outweigh his choice in accessories?

George's Paul Stuart suit with folded white handkerchief

trumps a bolo any day, and the decision is made. So long, Tim, see you at the town dock.

Don't let this happen to you! Careful selection of your children's schools, proper dress, and the right career will push you ahead of the Tims of this world and lock you into the ideal suburban lifestyle.

# Sports and Leisure Activities

We are what we play, so recreational pursuits must be selected with care. Adult males sail, golf, smite a tennis ball, and engage sporting clays. They do not race powerboats, but the discomfort of sailing, alas, is still with us, particularly on the coasts. Women shop, although tennis, jogging, and golf (weekday tee-offs only, so as not to disturb the road warriors when they come home on the weekend) are permitted. The entire family heli-skis. We do not fish, in salt water or fresh, unless by fly rod or from a deep-sea private charter sailing from an obscure, distant location; belly floats in the local fishing hole just won't do. Bicycling on anything other than a custom road or mountain bike costing at least $3,000 is strictly prohibited, unless we're on a bed-and-breakfast tour of France, in which case we may utilize $1,500 cruisers; after all, the friends we encounter will all be similarly mounted, so we'll simply shrug and murmur, with just a trace of embarrassment, "When in Rome. . . ." And besides, the discomfort will add to the adventure and enhance our party stories back home: "It only had twenty-four gears!"

## YOUR MOUNTAIN BIKE
**$4,500 Hand-Built Off the Shelf · $6,500+ with the Components You Rightly Deserve**

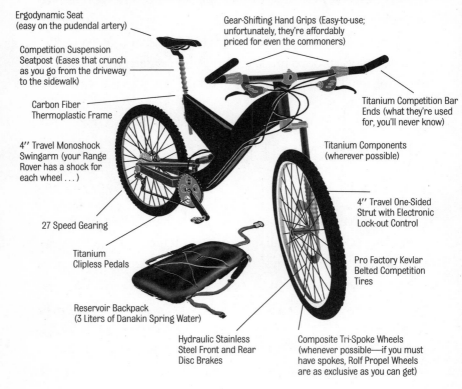

Ergodynamic Seat
(easy on the pudendal artery)

Competition Suspension
Seatpost (Eases that crunch
as you go from the driveway
to the sidewalk)

Carbon Fiber
Thermoplastic Frame

4" Travel Monoshock
Swingarm (your Range
Rover has a shock for
each wheel . . . )

27 Speed Gearing

Titanium
Clipless Pedals

Reservoir Backpack
(3 Liters of Danakin Spring Water)

Hydraulic Stainless
Steel Front and Rear
Disc Brakes

Gear-Shifting Hand Grips (Easy-to-use;
unfortunately, they're affordably
priced for even the commoners)

Titanium Competition Bar
Ends (what they're used
for, you'll never know)

Titanium Components
(wherever possible)

4" Travel One-Sided
Strut with Electronic
Lock-out Control

Pro Factory Kevlar
Belted Competition
Tires

Composite Tri-Spoke Wheels
(whenever possible—if you must
have spokes, Rolf Propel Wheels
are as exclusive as you can get)

# EXERCISE

Next to making money, exercise is the most hallowed activity we can engage in. Sweaty exertion has taken the place of church attendance in the new suburbs. Women, who by law must be no shorter than five foot ten and weigh not more than one hundred and five pounds, are required to jog in the rain, attend their health club at least three times weekly from ten until one-thirty, and wear Lycra spandex at all times during those same hours the rest of the week. The old suburban custom of Father arriving home from work and escaping the children by crawling into a scotch bottle has been replaced. Now he retreats to his gym in the master-bedroom suite each evening, reappearing only to kiss the children good night. On weekends, Father must take his oldest male child to the sports club, where the two of them will join other father-son teams for a rowdy but manly game of basketball, and then meet Mom and the daughters for take-out Starbucks and . . . shopping.

The best health clubs and personal trainers are those to which admittance is gained by invitation; YWCA aerobics courses, open to all, lack the cachet of Lotte Berk's classes of ten, and who would possibly want a personal trainer who didn't conduct body-fat and lung-capacity tests to select his clientele? Until you are capable of meeting Ms. Lotte's and Herr Rudolph's stringent standards governing fat ratio and circulatory rate, you will want to use the private services of a personal trainer in your home, as well as that of a masseuse (a male masseur is perfectly acceptable, so long as you have confidence in his discretion). This phase of body development must be passed through quickly, lest you be trapped forever among the cellulite queens of the lower classes. Diligence, girls!

# TOOLS, EQUIPMENT, AND GEAR

*"Sell a man a fish and eat for a day. Sell him*
*a bicycle and dine forever on the accessory sales."*

—LAO-TZU, 551 B.C.

The best part about being rich today is all the great toys we get to play with, most of which are handmade. We shop in London for the best English garden tools and shotguns, at the pro shop for custom golf clubs, Pedal & Paddle for that $20,000 titanium bicycle, and Fur, Fish, and Fin for the quadra-boron-graphite 2-weight fly rod handcrafted by an evil-smelling old man in Idaho. When descending to the world of ready-made, we never drop too far; we buy only top of the line, which means Bosch hand tools, Patagonia fleece (six times more expensive than Lands' End's identical product and worth every penny of it), and canvas "stand-up" shorts. In every store, in every catalog, there will always be a price hierarchy. Automatically select the most expensive and, unless you're in the wrong store or wrong catalog (L. L. Bean, for instance, instead of Patagonia, Sears (ha ha ha) instead of the Sharper Image), you'll do just fine.

Remember, it's not just a piece of equipment we're buying, it's a lifestyle. A custom bike demands special shoes, gloves, jerseys, eight-panel Microsensor™ chamois shorts, and a variety of helmets to fit your mood. That fly rod demands company—not just other rods in other weights but English fishing vests, custom-made waders, surgical stainless steel hemostats, hats, flies, several types of line (floating, sinking, and neutral), tropical casting shirts with Coolmesh™ armpits, (fish) stomach extractors, global-positioning-satellite receivers, a Range Rover, and so forth. What use is a shotgun without a Hermès shell carrier? Or Mephisto shooting shoes? Or a Harris tweed via Orvis gentleman's shooting jacket? Or a pair of champion bird dogs? Or five thousand acres of Vermont farmland to grouse on?

You get the picture, and so do the establishments that cater to our needs. The proper way to shop these outdoor emporiums is identical to that used in ordinary retail stores: hold your platinum card lightly between the index and second finger and gently wave in the direction of the objects you desire. Without looking at price tags (the stores we shop in don't use them anyway) drawl, "I'll take one of those, three of those in blue, two of these, and six of those. Deliver them to my house this afternoon." The key here is to remain absolutely casual, betraying no concern that you're charging $35,000 of, say, lawn furniture or tennis equipment. Your peers around you will recognize you as a fellow player and that, as the ad says, is priceless.

# ADVENTURING

Danger is in. Not real danger, of course; no one lets Americans participate in truly risky behavior, because we sue when we get hurt, but a whole market has sprung up to meet our need to spice up our lives and look, to our friends, as though we're risking life and limb. Fly-fishing through Patagonia? Go for it! You'll float down a smooth river in large, double-hulled rafts, fishing for huge, wild fish that no one makes you toss back, and be preceded the whole way by an army of servants. These people motor ahead of you, set up a large banquet for lunch, then clean everything up and speed by you again to establish a tent city for your evening dining and entertainment pleasure. Equitour will take you riding through Tibet on Thoroughbreds, house you in triple-sized yurts, and never serve you a single drop of curdled ghee. Every outdoor entrepreneur with the least bit of acumen has focused on our need for this kind of fun, with the result that we can go rafting, climbing, photo-safariing—you name it—in complete luxury and safety.

Hunting lodges and dude ranches used to provide all that we needed in the way of manly outdoor adventure, but hanging around peeled-log main cabins, sloshing scotch, and telling raunchy jokes is no longer acceptable. Instead, try one of the new resorts that offer "soft adventure" at its best. Your water will be triple-filtered, the staff (a one-to-one ratio of employee to guest) trained to distinguish between glasses for red and white wine, and your guided excursions will never take you out overnight. A jungle triathlon will be followed up by a gourmet dinner, a river ride, complete with a guide-belayed drop down ancient sinkholes, by a private session with a masseuse. *Everyone* has hunted elk before; your goal is to do something unique—these resorts will accomplish that for you. Expensive, naturally, but the best always is.

# BOATS

The old Prep fixation on all things nautical is rapidly giving way to a passion for golf; after all, business simply can't be transacted when host and guests are heeled sideways in a twisted cock-

## Mommy Trips on Lake Titicaca

*From a press release announcing a new travel service offered by Unleashed Adventures. Not one word has been changed.*

Our aim is to create women-only adventure trips that challenge us physically and mentally. We've all done Paris, various spa trips, and the usual family vacations to Florida, Nantucket or Antigua. But this is different. There's really nothing like adventuring with a group of like-minded women to some far-off exotic destination. A nice change of pace from the camaraderie we share in our car pool lines, gyms and coffee shops. There's something about trading in our Lily dress, Gucci loafers and black headband for a pair of synthetic long underwear, Tevas, grabbing a duffle bag, and heading out the door.

It's a rare opportunity to leave our care-giving roles behind and find ourselves being the ones cared for by talented guides who set up our tents, carry our packs, prepare our food, and help us with our boo-boos. On the cultural level, we've established relationships with the U.S. Ambassadors in each country we visit, and we'll have a welcoming reception there before we begin our adventure. In October, Donna Hrinack, U.S. Ambassador to Bolivia, will accompany us as we kayak on Lake Titicaca, and Patricia Cepeda, wife of U.S. Ambassador to Chile John O'Leary, will join our January program for the entire journey. The majority of our clientele are mothers - the count on the last trip was 43 children left behind with their dads, a marvelous opportunity for that all-important bonding!

The adventure bug has certainly bitten us and hope you will join us in our adventures. —Diane Terry, Unleashed Adventures, Greenwich

Wild, crazy readers can reach Diane at UnleashedA@aol.com

pit, ankle-deep in tossed cookies, their ears pressed just inches from blisteringly cold salt water. Nonetheless, there are still boat people of influence, and you may find it necessary to expose yourself to this foolish sport. Here are a few tips:

Bigger is better. To make the proper statement, the minimum length for a boat is fifty-two feet, if powered by sail, and eight-five feet for a motor yacht. Fishing boats are the exception: fifty feet will do, so long as they sport a tuna tower half as high as the boat is long. There is only one brand for sailboats—Hinckley—but we have more latitude in selecting our motor yacht, and can buy almost anything if it costs enough.

Accessorize, accessorize, accessorize. You spent the million, million and a half for the basic hull; now you'll want teak decks ($50,000 and up) GPS navigational systems ($75,000 to ?—ask the Pentagon), carbon fiber, stowaway masts for Hinckleys, the current hot interior decorator working his magic down below, Ralph Lauren–designed matching crew uniforms (especially when your children comprise the crew), entertainment systems that duplicate those in your home—you get the picture. Don't fret if your decorator lays an egg; you'll be trading up at least once each season, so you won't have to put up with the wrong color fabric for more than ninety days.

You will require a professional captain and his mate—known on dry land as his girlfriend—to deliver your boat to its cruising grounds, Tortola via Bermuda in winter and Maine in summer (for you Westies, that's Cabo and Mazatlán, winter, San Juan Islands, summer). This pair will not only make certain that your boat is ready and waiting for your impromptu visits but the mate will also cook and clean and the captain will teach you how to handle the damn thing. If you slam into the dock while maneu-

vering to pick up your passengers, any captain worth his salt will quickly grab the wheel and apologize, loudly, for his clumsiness. Discretion and confidentiality are the watchwords of all successful owner's captains.

Power or sail? Fortunately, the tide has turned, and we need no longer suffer the agonies of tilted, cramped quarters aboard a sailing vessel. The better yacht clubs have long since abandoned their prejudice against diesel turbos—they had to; they ran out of sailing applicants—and welcomed "stink potters" to their ranks. We who eschew salty discomfort can now wear Breton reds and ascoted blue blazers just like Walter Cronkite, only we can do so on the comfort of a spacious water-going motor home. And here's an easy answer for those unlucky few whose local yacht club insists on tradition: the Hinckley Picnic Launch. This charming little boat is fifty feet of gel-coated, water-jet-powered grace that draws just eighteen inches and zooms you around at forty-five knots. It lacks any sort of accommodations below, so its price of half a million dollars will convince even the worst old stick-in-the-mud that you're a yachter—someone willing to go to any lengths to fling unlimited amounts of money overboard. Buy one for town and another for the summer place and your entry into the best club at each location is assured.

Can't stand boats? Really can't stand them, so much so that the mere thought of stepping foot on one makes your face grow ashy-green? Buy yourself a (presalted) Mount Gay Rum hat—one that proclaims participation in Block Island race week is best, but any version will do. These little Breton red wonders, when properly faded, automatically place you in the ranks of the world's sailors. Stand near the walkway of any yacht club anywhere at the end of the day and watch the files of sailors trudging toward the bar. Every single one of them will be wearing his Mount Gay beanie, and if you, sagacious fellow that you are, were to drag your own cap from your hip pocket and set it loosely atilt on your own head, why, you could join that line of thirsty seamen. Then you'll stand elbow to elbow with them, swapping lies about rounding rights and reefing points and spinnaker hourglasses, all while safely protected from exposure by the alcoholic fog that settles down over the bar postrace, shrouding everyone in unintelligibility. You need never (hire someone to) scrape a barnacle again.

# WEEKEND HOMES

You will want several of these, scattered about the globe. The basic rule here is, the farther from your primary residence, the better. Beaver Creek, Colorado, is a preferred location for residents on either coast, from Chestnut Hill to Greenwich, Charleston to Beverly Hills. It's a long way from anywhere, so the expense of getting the family and friends there for just three days is quite impressive. By no means are you restricted to just one weekend home, of course, nor should you set your sights so low. A minimum of three, especially if one is in Provence or England's Lake District, can only improve your image among your peers.

# SUMMER HOMES

Everyone needs a summer home so that Mom and the kids can get away from grumpy old Dad and he, in turn, can get away from Mom. Your home can be in any number of places—in the East, East Hampton, Nantucket, or Martha's Vineyard, or even Litchfield County, Connecticut. The only criteria is that the house cost at least a million dollars and be surrounded by others costing just as much. This rules out all of Vermont and most of Maine, although certain sections of Bar Harbor can accommodate you. Cost need not be a concern in California, as even starter homes begin at the proper monetary threshold. Sante Fe is always popular, as are Jackson Hole in Wyoming and Sun Valley, Idaho, but the Big Sky country of Montana offers the best statement of rugged individualism. Mom and the kids will hate it—there are no restaurants or decent malls, and the celebrities are all hidden away on their million-acre ranches—but you, Dad, can take your fellow investment bankers fly-fishing. At least until the next fashion sport emerges, this piscatory adventuring is certainly worth the few pennies of jet fuel it may take for you to ship the rest of the family off to the Hamptons, leaving you in peace.

The proper size of a true vacation home varies; some of the smaller islands simply can't accommodate a mansion of the size we're used to but, generally, twenty thousand square feet is the minimum. (And why would you want a house on an island too small to permit this comfort range?) A currently popular theme for such houses is "Adirondack"–large palaces constructed of birch twigs and bark, and vaguely resembling the "great camps" built during the nineteenth century by robber barons vacationing in the Adirondack Mountains. Massive stone fireplaces and wrought-iron everything, including bear chandeliers, add just the right touch indoors. Of course, the nature of birch is to rot, and it rots even more quickly in the fetid air down South, but that hasn't stopped the popularity of these cabins, even in Georgia. And what of it? Ephemeral they may be, but what shouts "rich" better than a forty-thousand-square-foot disposable house?

For those readers who aren't willing to tolerate the bug infestation brought on by building homes from bark-covered logs, traditional construction is still acceptable in the better summer-resort locations. Make sure your home has a tennis court, free-form pool (even if, *especially* if, your home enjoys direct waterfront), and a kitchen indistinguishable from the one you just left in the suburbs (guaranteeing, of course, that it meets the size and priceline parameters discussed in the kitchen section of this book), and you need fear nothing from your neighbors.

Father gets to stay in the city during the week but is expected to either commute out each weekend (the men among us form plane syndicates for just this purpose) or spend the month of August with the family. Either way, he'll disappear to his club in the country for however long his stay lasts, appearing only at evening, dressed in the lightest of wool trousers (blue), white shirt, cardigan, and loafers, to escort Mother back to the club for a private party.

We do not ask what Father does in the city, unescorted, but how does the rest of the family spend its three months in paradise? Again, just as in the suburbs, their lives will revolve around their club. Sailing and golf lessons for the children, scheduled play dates with their peers, and illicit drinking at night, swilling a concoction assembled from the liquor cabinets of their parents or, in the more modern families, downing kegs ordered by Dad from the local supplier. Mother's routine is the same, but she will not usually combine rye with gin and she doesn't take sailing lessons; the women of suburbia do not sail, ever. Time that might have been wasted on this activity is invested instead in sunbathing and trading real estate stories.

We do not go on family excursions without at least one au pair, and this added presence does so much to enrich the summer experience. Not only will she provide chauffeur services for the children, but her own late-night adventures are sure to spark memorable visits to the police station and humorous anecdotes about sandy bedsheets and naked lifeguards escaping from the master bedroom when Mom and Dad return from the club. These experiences will be best enjoyed a few years after Lydia returns to North Dakota.

Naming the summer home is a questionable practice. If you feel you must, try to avoid the obvious. Seawinds, Summerbreeze, and, God help us, Casablanca are beyond the pale. Choose an indecipherable Scottish word or steal the name of an established

English manor and explain that you have such fond memories of dear Uncle Adrian's Lake District estate that you just had to bring the name home from overseas.

# VACATIONS

We can't spend all our time at the summer place or weekend home, of course; we'll be seen as paupers. Suburban life demands excursions to many new and different places, all expensive and all spent in the company of PLUs—People Like Us. The old standbys like Paris and London are always acceptable, but here's your chance to be creative. While we don't do Disney World, Dollywood, or Myrtle Beach, we can and do frequent the new breed of dude ranches in the summer, Vail or Sun Valley in the winter, and, always, the Caribbean—no Club Meds, please. Private school vacations last two weeks, and when you have children of the appropriate age, you will schedule your vacation trips accordingly: one week skiing, preferably at Beaver Creek, then one week in the sunny Caribbean. Never the reverse, and never two weeks in one climate. By the way, we never ski in Vermont if we can help it; it's too accessible for easterners and, regardless of state of residence, far too icy and cold.

Exotic locales are ideal; in fact, you will by choice prefer destinations your friends must use a map to locate (they will do so in private, naturally, after first assuring you that they were planning the same trip themselves), so long as there is a 100 percent guarantee of your safety. The English may court danger, but not the better class of Americans. That means no trips to Cuba and certainly not Africa, if it entails wandering through dark jungles filled with hostile black warriors. Photo safaris, safely limited to the secure zones of Kenya, may be planned, but for our class the very best trip of all, one that combines distance with complete safety, is Antarctica. Other than a grumpy penguin or two, there will be nothing there to threaten our serenity.

No children? Or, better yet, are your children on their own art-appreciation tour of France with their private tutor? Then consider the adventure resorts discussed above. They're no more dangerous than a dude ranch, but they *seem* to be, and that makes it all so much more fun.

## SUMMER CAMP

Since we stopped shipping our sons off to the military, Outward Bound has prospered as a toughening agent for our capitalist warriors-to-be. A month of being flung off cliffs and dunked in cold water has a bracing effect on any child, particularly one who's been flagrantly "experimenting" at prep school. It may do no good at all, of course, but in the unfortunate event that Brandon's retail drug activities make the local police blotter, we can hold our heads high and say, "I just can't imagine how Outward Bound failed so badly."

But what about the rest of our children, the ones doing so well at school, the ones who spend every waking hour of the school year studying, practicing, and doing that volunteer community service so necessary for college admission? They deserve a reward for their hard work, and the children's camp industry has transformed itself for just that purpose.

If you went to camp at all, you probably remember moldy, leaky log cabins or tents, with spiders in every crevice and stinky old latrines posing a four-hundred-yard challenge for nocturnal

visits. Put away those memories and relax; today's camps bear the same relationship to yesterday's as your custom-crafted road bicycle does to the three-speed Raleigh you pedaled to third grade. We're talking gourmet meals, served up by $100,000-per-season chefs, and air-conditioned cabins, arachnid-free, with personal bathrooms and spas for each camper. You can also take for granted hot-water showers poolside (no mucking about in lakes, which probably have icky things like fish in them, for our children), DVD players by each bed and in every cabin's living room, maid service, the finest of psychiatric care for dealing with separation problems, drug and alcohol counseling, and sophisticated sports-training programs coached by the top stars in each field.

Our first step in selecting a camp is to hire a camp consultant. With that help in hand, we set about matching our desires for our children with the many, many enriching opportunities available. Did Amanda enjoy her ninth-birthday party when you flew her and her friends to Antigua for a weekend of scuba diving? Then book her on a Windstar Adventure, where she'll cruise the Caribbean aboard a million-dollar yacht, hone her diving skills, and enjoy shopping excursions at all the best islands. Does Robert take the Hummer out for surreptitious late-night excursions through the canyons? Don't discourage his initiative; he'll be sixteen in two years, and how will you control him then? Send him

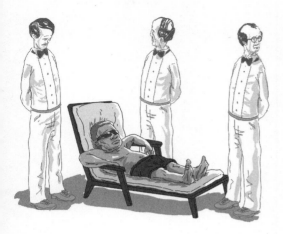

instead to Hummer Camp, where, equipped with night-vision goggles, luxurious safari tents, servants, and one of those fine chefs, he'll explore the deserts of Utah, camping under the stars and learning the driving skills he'll need in the busy world of Los Angelean highways.

From Kenya to California to Maine, kid adventures abound; one of them is sure to offer just the right environment for your child. They'll travel in comfort and style and be treated with the respect due them as scions of your distinguished bloodline. Send them off to see the world and forget about them; you'll get back an even more perfect child.

# Chapter 10

# PERSONAL CARE

# HAIR CARE

Suburban men can get by with modest amounts of professional attention; a manicurist is often provided by the firm, and a weekly haircut (at Alphano's Barbershop for Gentlemen, *not* Four Guys Named Fred), a regular exercise program, and minor plastic surgery every decade should keep you looking fit from your thirties until old age—say, fifty-five. Women have a more difficult time.

One of the first major decisions thrust upon a new suburbanite is the question of hair care. Does she stay with her stylist in the city or dare risk the less skilled ministrations offered in the wilderness? One can certainly find a hairdresser willing to charge us $400 in the suburbs, but majority opinion suggests that you stick with the city, for one very important reason: class. Keeping on your urban hairdresser sends a strong message that you have the leisure time to devote one day a week to travel to the city and that you have a capable staff at home, large enough to manage the many crises that always happen when the Mistress leaves her abode. It also affords an opportunity to shop at those little boutiques that, no matter how advanced the suburbs become, can never be truly duplicated in a rural setting.

Regardless of where she has her hair pampered, the new suburbanite will be reassured to learn that all the other critical services are readily available in the wilds. Any number of salons will do a competent job of bronzing, for instance. Trained staff will carefully exfoliate your entire body, then a team of reconstructionists will tenderly smooth bronzing gel all over your body, creating the perfect tan. The results will be indistinguishable from those obtained at urban salons.

## DOCTORS

Laser treatment for the removal of nasty leg hair is offered at any respectable dermatologist's office and, in the suburbs, there are almost as many dermatologists as there are orthodontists.

We tend to stay with our original psychiatrists, but family counselors for the children are best if located in our town. It's all very well to have the driver take Emily off to the big city, but it does cut into all those other after-school activities colleges demand these days, and what's the point of mental nurturing if the end result is a rejection from Harvard?

## NUTRITIONISTS

We all need them in order to avoid starving to death on our grapefruit and endive diets. These happy guides will supply us with the kelp pills, blue algae, and megavitamins so essential for maintaining skin tone while our bodies are shutting down. Our daughters will be introduced to their own personal nutritionists at age seven; boys, unless they're obese, can wait until they have wives of their own to bring home samples and useful advice.

# Day Spas

A wonderful way to pamper yourself after a tough week of getting everyone ready for the new school year or organizing the charity auction. Noel is just one such provider, but you should find the same basic services wherever you go. Report in at 9:30 A.M., doff your clothes, and let yourself be wrapped in a thirsty, plush terry-cloth robe. Surrender yourself to the process: steam bath, massage, mud bath, another massage, pedicure, manicure, facial massage, shampoo, haircut, more steam bath, another massage, consultation with nutritionist, then go. Your husband may grumble when he receives a bill for all of this, but, really: if you left it up to him, he couldn't possibly spend all the money he's bringing in. Go out and enjoy, dears.

# Chapter 11

# READY, SET, SHOP!

# RETAIL

We don't like malls. In the newer suburbs there may be no choice, but then, that is why we don't move to the newer suburbs. No, the proper place to shop is still Main Street, whether it's the Plaza in Sante Fe or Rodeo Drive or Elm Street in New Canaan. This is where we'll meet our friends and neighbors; this is where we'll pay top dollar. Fortunately, you will find all of your favorite mall retailers present on Main Street—Ralph Lauren, Saks, Bodyworks, even Gaps for Kids are all waiting for you in the great outdoor bazaar that comprises the new downtown.

One must never go shopping with a particular item in mind—that's an errand, and that's why you have servants. Suburban shopping is a little like Justice Potter Stewart's definition of obscenity: you will know what you need when you see it. This sort of expedition is always done in the company of one or two, no more, of your friends. Lunch breaks are taken either at the best restaurants or your club, and will be eaten in a cacophony of shrilling beepers and cell phones while you all rearrange your children's play dates for that day.

For clothing purchases, the best of us will insist upon the services of our own personal shoppers—these ladies will not only mewl over us like any ordinary sales assistant, they will also place surreptitious calls around our husbands to alert us when a new Armani suit "that's just perfect for you" is coming in. The right gal, one who mixes obsequiousness with fashion savvy, just guarantees a glorious shopping experience.

We do not comparison shop, we do not read *Consumer Reports*, and we do not care about price, except to shy from items that are too inexpensive for our household. The question for us is not "How much does it cost?" or "Is it the best value for the money?" but, rather, "What do my *friends* own?" And remember, the next

time some bit of trash shoots you a disdainful glare as you load those nice little bundles of split-birch firewood, at six dollars a log, into the Mercedes wagon, that six dollars to *him* is six cents to you. Would he fill up his battered pickup truck with six-cent bundles of fuel? Of course he would! Go right ahead with your purchase and pay him no heed.

If you must economize, do so in an appropriate way. Purchase a $9,000 couture dress for the charity ball on Friday, and on Saturday morning send it back via one of your servants. This practice drives many small retailers out of business, we do it so often, but there will always be more of their type to serve our needs and, besides, won't we look clever when we recount the tale at our exercise class Monday morning?

A little embarrassed by some of your purchases? Does spending $2,800 for a plump Legends eiderdown pillow from the Company Store seem just a tad excessive when there are starving children somewhere in the world? (You may have seen them on your adventure tour in Peru—those little girls you envied for their stick figures, for instance.) Well, the heck with it. If we want it, then we need it, and we're entitled. Still doubtful? Listen to that eminent sociologist James B. Twitchell, author of *Lead Us into Temptation: The Triumph of American Materialism*. Twitchell explains that expensive purchases are a form of healing, a way to say to ourselves, "I'm worth it, I deserve it, and they owe me big time." You bet, Jim. We *are* worth it, and no one else is; we're special.

## GROCERIES

There are A&Ps and Piggly Wigglys in the suburbs, presumably, but we don't patronize them; we visit the specialty gourmet-food stores instead. Stores like Hay Day and Fresh Fields, Harris Teeter, Taylor's of Harrogate, and, although it is becoming far closer to mass merchandising than we like, Starbucks. At these stores we will find such rarities as the $10 strawberry, the $500 pound of green tea, and specially prepared, herb-encrusted delicacies for the busy mom, who can call on her cell phone as she speeds from her aerobics class and have an entire meal ready for pickup at $60 per portion (certainly justifiable, when one considers the savings in not using the Garland gas stove to cook). One can shoppe at any of these fine emporiums without fear of encountering and, even worse, accidently purchasing an inappropriate product. No Procter & Gamble soaps or shampoos on these stores' shelves—it's pure Crabtree & Evelyn, and Tom's of Maine Natural Toothpaste. Pick what you like—you won't find anything that might embarrass you when some nosy guest peeks into your cupboards.

## HOUSEHOLD WARES

Now that all of the better suburbs have passed laws banning Woolworths and Wal-Marts from our streets, we can buy everything we need at huge markups from tidy, little hardware shops and boutiques. You will love it. The salesclerks in such stores understand the fawning servility that we expect, and they dish it out in huge dollops of obsequiousness. No sullen shirkers here! You'll be greeted at the door by a hand-wringing sales associate who will trot behind you during your visit, meekly noting down everything you want, as you point an imperious finger and command, "One of those, two of those, and give me that, in tan." Just the sight of them scrambling to obey is enough to lift the spirits of any jaded shopper.

# SOURCES

The Old Money knows of secret little places in the city where one may buy entire kitchens, jewels, home furnishings, couture clothing, and so on, at wholesale. New Money is far more efficient, and never exposes the Lady of the House to unsavory environs. We discover sources by listening carefully to our friends and learning who their friends are. "I'm lunching tomorrow with the head of Sotheby's" or "Do let me know the next time you need jewelry—Paloma Picasso is little Hayward's godmother" will be all you need to avoid getting dirty while still enjoying the same bargains the older types do.

Mind you: you must be careful, if you mention a bargain price, to also mention how you got it. New suburbia places no value on personally scouting out dark alleys, and if that's the best you can do, say you paid 110 percent over retail and earn your friends' admiration that way. But if Walter Hoving himself escorted you through Tiffany's, helped you pick out just the right fifteen-diamond necklace, and then insisted that you pay no more than wholesale, well, that's appropriate for public disclosure. In fact, it's mandatory.

# Chapter 12

# CHARITIES AND ASSOCIATIONS

The real women of suburbia stay at home—no two-income families here! But when gourmet-coffee-shop meetings with other mothers grow stale, when the body refuses another session with the personal trainer, and when Saks Fifth Avenue opens its doors to the general public for a markdown sale, something must fill the void. Charities await.

In the olden days of the 1970s the Junior League provided all that one needed to fill in the odd hours between bridge games at the club and cocktail hour, but no longer. Almost anyone can join the League now, and the resulting loss of exclusivity has severely diminished its prestige. The smart set still belongs, if only out of habit, but the real action can be found by serving on boards of trustees and directorships, where who your husband is still matters. Art museums, the Boys and Girls Club (for fund-raising purposes only—our children do *not* participate in Boys and Girls Club activities), and environmental organizations (a little too brainy for most of us, but Radcliffe graduates like them) are just a few of the many opportunities you will have to serve your fellow suburbanites. If you will ask discretely among your friends, you will soon learn which organization currently resides on the peak of Prestige Mountain.

What will you do on these boards? What any women's group does: raise money. You'll help plan charity balls, antique shows, and house tours. You will participate in that most important of all social functions, the fund-raiser auction, where Labrador puppies, dinner for two at your favorite restaurant, vacations on St. Barts or Nevis, Abercrombie & Kent luxury barge tours through the Bordeaux region, excursions on the twenty-passenger *Sea Goddess* and front-row seats for little Cooper's graduation will each be auctioned off for $25,000 above retail. A parking space in the school lot for that senior you're so proud of can usually be won for around $6,000, representing the best bargain of the night. In all these events, you'll be with your very best friends, and you will love it. Your husband's role is simpler; he simply dresses up in his tux, complains as he struggles with his cummerbund that he'll never attend another function like this again, and then arrives at whatever auction your group is conducting and bids drunkenly and extravagantly on the toys you're peddling. The greater the multiple between what he bids versus the retail price of the item, the greater the prestige, so make certain his checking account is in shape for the evening. After all, his performance is a direct reflection on you.

# Chapter 13

# CATASTROPHIC ILLNESS AND CALAMITY

Bad things happen to even the best people, sadly, but here in the suburbs we pride ourselves on our ability to cope. Even the shyest mother is willing to face up to the illnesses ravaging her children and herself, and discuss them with her friends. This includes problems such as attention deficit disorder, selecting the proper nutritionist to deal with the eating disorders of our children, the heartbreak of young Victoria's three-pound gain during her latest growth spurt, Tucker's unmet need for untimed SATs, emergency administration of growth hormones to Clayton so that he can be taller than his parents, and so on. Emergency plastic surgery can be talked about bravely: tummy tucks, breast lifts, and liposuction. Go ahead and reach out for help—your friends will steer you to just the right surgeon to reduce those hips and tighten your breasts in time to bare all on St. Barts.

And, oddly enough, serious diseases come in clusters in the suburbs. One private day school was recently forced to cancel its entire fall sports program after a local doctor detected a serious, life-threatening heel disorder among every single boy who played on the soccer team. The campus presented an eerily disturbing scene after the good doctor had finished his examinations and ordered three hundred young athletes onto crutches and into specially supplied (fortunately, the doctor was able to manufacture them himself) orthopedic shoes. You can imagine the support network the mothers formed to get them all through that crisis!

## INJURIES

All of us strive to eliminate the risks of suburban life, but accidents can happen. Use foresight here to minimize risk: one mother reports, "I'd never let Treynor play golf—I heard that Terrence Coulter was struck in the head by a ball so hard that he actually had to see a doctor!" If our boy runs into another on the playing fields of St. Mark's, the result is never a "goose egg"—it's a full-blown concussion, by God, and something should have been done to prevent it. When, despite our best efforts, something awful does happen, we sue. Keep that smart lawyer's card handy at all times.

# ALCOHOLISM

There are no alcoholics in the suburbs, only an unfortunate few with "a drinking problem," but it's getting increasingly difficult to figure out who they are. So many of us claim to be off the sauce until the marathon that mere public abstinence won't reveal the lushes among us. You'll want to know, of course, so here's a tip for ferreting out the true alkie: watch for him at the edge of the party, sipping coffee, puffing on a cigarette, and looking bored. Now *there's* a drunk! Tell your friends.

# DIVORCE

In the suburbs, divorce instantly transforms women into pariahs. Suddenly single with three kids and a house to maintain, they are assumed to be hunting for a replacement gutter cleaner and, as such, are no longer welcome at the homes and parties of their still married friends. With their former husband's consent, they may remain members at their country club but only as a "Class B," subject to an annual behavior review. One unpleasant poolside squabble and that's it. It is a solitary life, in a constricted social circle made up of other divorcées and widows, but there are certainly new opportunities for volunteer activity. For those who have neglected the art of reading, now is an appropriate time to locate the town library. As for employment, most suburban towns have enacted ordinances that require divorcées to work as real estate agents. This workfare program pushes the cosseted dears out of the house while diluting the earnings of the other agents, thereby keeping most of those agents' annual income below a million dollars; it can be quite embarrassing when a member of the trades earns more than the junior dot-coms in town. Lesson for women: stand by your man, at least until you have another one in the wings. On the other hand, there are some awfully attractive carpenters in the suburbs, so if you're sure of your alimony, you just might want to order up a bit of renovation work!

Divorced men fare a little better, although they, too, will be banished from the homes of their former friends by angry wives threatened by the act of abandonment. Men are more likely to remarry, probably because they have a wider pool in which to

search, and once safely attached to a new woman and busy procreating new toddlers to attend class plays with, they will soon recreate a new social world in which to operate.

# UNEMPLOYMENT

Restructuring happens, and the sudden disappearance of January's multimillion-dollar bonus can upset even the best household budgets, but cheer up! There are dozens of tricks we can use to keep up appearances while the head hunters work their magic. These include:

• Bags and packages: It's easy to sew designer labels on T. J. Maxx specials, and the hospital thrift shop is a fine place for bargains. A few rough moments can be expected when you encounter your garment's original donor at the charity auction, but smile and deny—always deny.

Remember also that it's what's outside that counts in many areas. Johnnie Walker Blue Label costs $350 per liter, John Begg runs $17.50 the quart, and they both come in bottles; a funnel costs 49¢, and you know what to do from here. Here's a hint for dinner parties: A&P charges $2 for a pound of coffee, the Precious Few Gourmet charges $15. Both come in paper sacks, and if you're worried about

spilling a few grounds on your granite kitchen countertop, for Christ's sake, dry off that funnel.

• Newspapers: Cancel your subscriptions to *Wall Street Journal* and the *New York Times,* but save one of each to place on the driveway before you sleep. Retrieve them each morning, put them back at night, and no one will ever notice your little financial embarrassment.

• Gasoline: Run the Beemer on low-grade swill and blame the sputtering results on Marcus, who's closed his boutique repair shop and returned to Italy for a few months.

• Private school tuition: Stick Orthwaith in public school for a semester or two and inform your friends that he's studying in a program for gifted students at Oxford. This may seem an invitation for disaster by discovery, but we assure you, your friends do not enter public schools—ever.

• Tenants: Only in the direst emergency, and only if your tenant can convincingly inform party guests that he's occupying the master bedroom as a special favor from you, his most favorite aunt.

• Entertain at your club: Because of the nasty practice of "posting" members delinquent in their bills, club fees and charges must be, and are, kept current long after credit cards have been canceled and mortgages declared in default. When you have to entertain— and in the suburbs, not to entertain is an open admission of financial difficulty—do so at your club and charge it to your tab. If in doubt as to your status, drop by earlier in the day to make certain your name hasn't been added to the lobby bulletin board by an officious treasurer.

• Early retirement: Remember, your husband hasn't been fired; he's taken early retirement. This implies great wealth, and if hubby is lucky enough to find gainful employment again, you can simply explain that he grew bored with his new life as a member of the idle rich.

Sadly, none of the tricks described above will fool your own children. They will detest you when you're poor and call you a loser to your face. Of course, they learned at your knee, but it will still hurt. Go find a job.

# Chapter 14

# OLD AGE AND RETIREMENT

*"Our fifties will be the new thirties."*

—(A HOPEFUL) MARY CHAPIN CARPENTER, AGE FORTY-TWO

It's all very well to retire at forty-nine, as so many of us will, but the banausic life does not inspire much in the way of creative self-reliance. If you're like the rest of us and have not read a book cover to cover since prep school but have spent your time since then exclusively generating and spending wealth, what are you to do with the years between retirement and enfeeblement? The answer, it often turns out, is nothing, so you'll scurry back to the ranks of the employed and serve as a consultant to the industry you just left. But what if no one wants your advice? What if they pushed you out of your job precisely because you had nothing to offer, because a twenty-two-year-old monkey can trade collateralized mortgage obligations every bit as well as you do, at far less cost? The sudden realization that nobody really depends on your sage counsel can be depressing, causing many male new suburbanites to sit alone in empty mansions wondering what the Retired Men's Association is all about and worrying about their prostates. Wives will stop in between club luncheons and personal-training sessions to ask you to run errands. The kids will call from college, occasionally, to ask for new cars and . . . that's it. That's your new life of ease.

It doesn't have to be that way, of course. You still have that magic elixir, money, and now's the time to use it. The same boards that welcomed your wife will invite you in with even more enthusiasm; after all, your wife was only brought in because she presented a pathway to your pocket. You are the real thing, and you should be able to easily fill up at least three nights a month and a few luncheon hours by this route. Add a club chairmanship on something like the reconfiguration of tee placements or, for you aging lawyers, revision of the bylaws, and a few more days will be occupied painlessly.

You can't write, but don't let that stop you from typing up your business memoirs, mixed with funny tales from the neighborhood and a few stale aphorisms, and submitting them to the publisher of your local Swells' magazine. He'll try to beg off, claiming, "Gee, the editor makes these decisions," but he owes you! If you didn't invite him to all those tent parties over the years, what would he have filled his pages with? If he won't relent, then cranky letters to the editor of the local paper will have to do for this artistic avenue.

Beware of making yourself too available for committee work or you will cheapen the currency. You must travel at least six months of the year. In your early fifties you should still be able to manage fishing trips to Patagonia, treks in the Himalayas, and Senior Outward Bound excursions. Take advantage of what's left of your energy and do all these things—it displays you at your virile best, still a captain of industry, even if your ship has gone on without you.

At some point, the ugly thought of a retirement community will flash across your mind, probably at the suggestion of your children, who think the mansion could be put to better work by

housing their growing families instead of two old grumps. Resist this like the plague! Your connections are here, in your town. People finally "know who you are," and the tremendous number of shop-counter scenes you staged to drive home that point will all be wasted if you leave and try to start again somewhere else. A home on Hobe Sound or in Palm Springs for the winter months is fine, as is a three-month stay in the Nantucket home, if you can get away with it (the children have other plans for that space, too). But giving up your home base is giving up on life, and fifty is too soon for that sad moment.

At sixty, of course, there's not much point in prolonging the battle, and you'll have to start investigating those retirement communities and assisted-living hotels that lurk so menacingly from the pages of *Modern Maturity*. Your life may not be quite over, but your time in the fast lane is. How does one adapt to this loss of prestige and independence? Which communities offer at least a vestige of pride and treat you like the entitled person you once were? These are questions for another book, and an older writer. Good luck in your somnolence: Whitney and I are out of here.

# ASK WHITNEY: ADVICE FOR NEW ARRIVALS

Dear Whitney:

We're expecting our first child, a boy, and gosh are we stumped for names! Our own family lines are a bit Eastern Europy for harmonious blending in our new town—can you just imagine sending young Gradstzdk to St. Alban's? Hoo! Obviously we can't use one of those name books by the supermarket cash register, so what do we do?

Dazed and Expecting
in Chevy Chase

# FROM THE DESK OF WHITNEY

Dear Chevy:

What do you do? Why, you write to me dear, as you have just done. Here are the currently acceptable names for our male offspring:

| | |
|---|---|
| Logan | Ashley |
| Whitney | Penn |
| Dillion | Cameron |
| Morgan | Lucas |
| Coulter | Deakin |
| Coleman | Cooper |
| Justin | Spencer |
| Zachary | Terrence |
| Liam | Bryce |
| Carter | Preston |
| Vaughn | Garrett |
| Brooks | Mackenzie |
| Brendon | Gordie |
| Bridges | Clayton |
| Tucker | Chase |
| Conor | Jarett |
| Trevor | Carlton |

And for females:

Alexandra

Ana

Amanda

Antoinette (never match with
    French surname—too ethnic)

Andrea

Ashley

Ariane

Brooke

Avery

Carolene

Camille (see warning above)

Davina

Courtney

Elissa

Emilie

Jessica

Gillian

Kathryn

Kaitlin

Kendell

Katrina

Laura

Kimberly

Leslie

Lauriston

Maisie

Mackenzie

Melinda

Megan

Mickelia

Melony

Renee

Nikia

Sasha

Shaye

Rosanda

Dear Whitney:

The children insist that we buy a pet and they tell me that, according to their peers, only a dog will do. Is this true? I worry that a dog will track mud all over our wall-to-wall carpeting and I would prefer something caged, like a guinea pig, or perhaps a nice ten-thousand-gallon saltwater aquarium. Must we buy a dog? If so, which breeds are on the current approved list? Portuguese water dogs? Beagles? Please rush your response, as the children at Miss Simpson's Academy can be ruthless in their teasing.

Sincerely,

Shedding Hair in Katonah

# From the Desk of Whitney

Dear Shedding:

Of course you need a pet, and yes, your children are right—the only acceptable pet for the suburbs is a dog. Guinea pigs and other rodents are simply too outré, and an aquarium of the size you mention suggests exuberant enthusiasm, something in which we do not indulge. You will want a dog, but not just any dog. Beagles remind us of midwestern rabbit hunts and haven't been acceptable in proper circles since the 1950s. Portuguese water dogs were certainly au courant in the late '80s, but their cachet has waned as their popularity has increased. Welsh Spaniels are an intriguing new find, and that old standby the Lhasa apso still retains an exclusivity which endears. You may, if you must, be a teensy bit boring and choose a Labrador—yellow or chocolate is best, but black provides an interesting color contrast for the suburbs. The only requirements for this latter breed is that you must buy one with both English and American bloodlines, all properly documented, and you must procure the puppy from a breeder in either Rhode Island or Bridgehampton—no exceptions here. Although I sense from your letter that you would never consider such a thing, I will use this opportunity to remind other readers that we do not "do" Adopt-a-Dog.

Golden retrievers are still popular, despite or because of their brains having been bred out—many new suburbanites appreciate a combination of stunning good looks and low mental capacity because it's less threatening. Choose any of the recommended dogs and your children will be able to hold their heads high at Miss Simpson's Academy. As for mud and hair on the carpeting, well, that's why you bought the green Super Suction Miele model for your maids to use, wasn't it? Tell them to do so.

Dear Whitney:

The other day at exercise class another mother made what I thought was a rude comment about my eight-carat diamond ring. Should I continue to wear it during class? It was presented to me by my husband on my fortieth birthday—only he could know how to cheer a girl up on that awful occasion—and I'm rather fond of it. If I do wear it, how should I respond the next time an envious classmate attacks?

Smarting but Sparkling in Bel Air

# FROM THE DESK OF WHITNEY

Dear Smarty:

You didn't say so, but I suspect this vulgar woman spotted you at the YWCA. It is precisely to avoid this sort of thing that we prefer private exercise classes, where we all wear our diamonds and where, frankly, my dear, eight carats is considered to be something more suitable for our daughter's sweet sixteen than a gift for a mature woman. Go back to your husband and demand better! You needn't respond at all to the savagery displayed by that charwoman; your job is to enjoy, not defend—switch clubs and relax. Don't forget, by the way, that "always right" item, the diamond tennis bracelet. When worn on the courts with smallish diamond earrings—two and a half to three and a half carats is just right—you can be confident that you're well dressed and up to date. Enjoy!

*Dear Whitney:*

*As the mother of a newborn, I'm a little confused by an invitation I just received, inviting little Dylan to a play date six months from now. Frederick and I are new to the suburbs, and we do want to fit in, but should I really commit our son to a snack-time engagement so far in advance when he doesn't even know the child?*

*Gnawing Fingernails
in Chestnut Hill*

# From the Desk of Whitney

Dear Gnawing:

Your child's already been born and you don't have an appointment diary booked? Shame on you and shame on your parenting class for not warning you of this necessity. You're lucky that young Dylan's been invited anywhere on such short notice—your husband must be one important man! Yes, Gnawing, you must accept the invitation on Dylan's behalf, and you must immediately purchase a five-year planner and begin booking the rest of his schedule now. All of our children are perfect, but that perfection must be safeguarded and nurtured by carefully selecting how every single minute of their first sixteen years is spent. There is no unscheduled time allowed in our world, so get at it, girl. You have certainly already enrolled Dylan in the proper Episcopal nursery school; stop by and pick up the directory of other prescient parents today. Then pull out your cellular and begin booking, not forgetting, meanwhile, to accommodate karate, dance, and hockey lessons, all of which will start in two and a half years. You've started late, but a diligent effort now may enable you to catch up. Good luck!

Dear Whitney:

Our daughter has met Mr. Perfect and a June wedding is planned. We're all just thrilled, of course—he's a Harvard MBA and his parents are People Like Us, but between Jennifer's requests and picking just the right location for the ceremony, I feel I'm drowning! Help!

Underwater in Charleston

# From the Desk of Whitney

Dear Charles:

You poor, wet dear. On this, what is possibly the most important social engagement of your career, of course you want everything to be perfect, and no wonder you feel at sea. There are just so many things to consider! Here's a lifeline.

The location for the wedding will be Nantucket or any of the best Maine islands; if you haven't already done so, buy a home up there now. A place so far from Charleston sets a nice tone, as you will be paying for the food, entertainment, and lodging of your closest one hundred friends (plus Dad's business "must invites"–the daughter's college friends can fend for themselves), so EXPENSIVE will seep out of the invitations.

Those invitations, of course, will be conveyed on Mrs. John L. Strong stationery–available at Barneys New York or at Mrs. Strong's own New York showroom from ten until four weekdays, *no* mail order! All of her exclusive product has deckled edging and costs $1,000 per hundred. So much more impressive than Crane's or Tiffany's, which can be had by anyone at $250 per.

Your photographer will charge $7,000, more if you insist (and I do hope you won't) on videotaping. Nelson Doubleday has a line on the priciest–call up the New York Mets front office and ask for Nelly, and be sure to tell him that Whitney sent you!

The Episcopal church on your island will be best, and the ceremony will be performed by the bride's hometown priest. If you or your daughter haven't been attending church on a

–2–

regular basis (and with today's busy schedules, who can?) now's the time for a generous contribution to the church retirement fund and a few dinner invitations.

The island's yacht club will provide a picturesque setting for the reception, particularly if you can rent the entire grounds and keep the casually dressed locals away. This may be difficult in Nantucket, but as the members there will all be dressed identically, you can tell your guests that they are part of the wait staff. (The apoplectic reaction of William Ogelthorpe III being directed to fetch a gin and tonic may well repay the entire cost in pure entertainment value.) Again, keep that checkbook handy and you should have no problem.

Unless you know and trust the local caterer, bring up yours from home. You won't have to put them up with your guests, of course, so lodging costs will be minimal—four to a room at the Holiday Inn will do nicely.

Our children often insist on a "rockin'" band for their entertainment and that of their friends. This is where we must put our Stubbs & Wooten–clad foot down, firmly, and remind the dear one just who exactly this wedding is for. A thirty-piece swing band is an acceptable compromise here.

There can never be enough champagne at these functions. Buy it by the truckload and please, please, please! don't attempt to economize on this essential nectar. No matter how carefully napkin-wrapped the bottle, no matter how

–3–

inebriated our friends may be become, the truth will out, and if you are caught serving Spanish or Californian pig swill, your life will be ruined forever.

You've waited years for this special day just for you—take care and enjoy!

Dear Whitney:

Our recently built home in the bucolic backwoods of this exclusive neighborhood is being attacked by hordes of thin blond women and old (albeit well-dressed) men, all on horseback, who claim a right to trespass along "trails immemorial." We've tried to stop them, of course, by having our men place, first, a stone wall and, later, concertina wire across the trail, but they persist! We can't see them (the trail in question lies in the rear of our fifty acres), but just knowing that someone is using our property is driving Hank and me crazy. How can we stop these equine fools without jeopardizing our application to the Field Club?

Restless in Bedford

# FROM THE DESK OF WHITNEY

Dear Restless:

Oh dear. First, immediately order your groundsmen to remove the obstacles, and then send invitations around to the entire riding circle for a "Huntsmen's Brunch" next Sunday. Hard as it is to believe, the Backcountry Swells still do exist and you, dear Restless, have inadvertently stumbled upon a nest of them. These people keep horses and think it grand fun to frolic over the property of others—a throwback to Socialist England, perhaps. Whatever their reasoning, the Swells can and do carry clout with the admissions committees of the various clubs, and a black ball from them dooms you—you'll never gain admittance to the club of your choice and you will have to move.

Once you get in, of course, it's another matter. Then pile up that concertina wire until you have a veritable symphony reaching to the skies. Prepare trap falls and punji pits, and station armed guards at the perimeter of your property. A few months of this, and a few unfortunate injuries to the lead riders, and you and your husband can relax in the knowledge that every inch of the property you bought and paid for is yours, all yours.

Dear Whitney:

Help! My daughter in Kent, Connecticut, just lost an election for team captain of her prep school's crew team. She'd promised me she'd win and I, naturally, announced the good news to all our friends. How can I possibly confess the truth: some scholarship girl from Iowa was more popular than my Gillian?

Crushed in Darien

# From the Desk of *W*hitney

Dear Crushed:

We must never forget to use our blessings from Christ when pursuing our goals. God's given you money for a purpose, and this is it. Call the headmaster at Kent immediately and get his price. A modern crewing shell costs $90,000, and Kent girls row nothing but castoffs from the boy's team. How many new boats will it take to put your girl in her proper place and shove that corn-fed, midwestern sow overboard? One? Five? Ten and a new boathouse? There's a price that will do the deal; your task is to find it. Remember, what happens here will determine what college your daughter attends, what type of man she will marry, and where she'll settle with her family. Unless you want to visit your grandchildren in Hartford, pick up that phone and call right now.

Dear Whitney:

(Sigh) Our neighbor insists on keeping peacocks in his backyard. The cock's calls wake Duncan and the children, the feathers float over onto our manicured grounds, and, all in all, it's just a mess! The zoning officer has informed me that poultry raising is a permitted use in this town (!), but I'm worried about our property values. What can I do to stop him?

Sleepless in Sonoma

Z Z Z Z z

# From the Desk of Whitney

Dear Sleepy:

Naturally, you will want to sue. And not with just any old firm, either. The old suburban law firms are useless for this sort of pest removal; the partners all belong to the same clubs as your neighbors, and as the result they play fuzzy-mitten law—cushy little depositions, scheduled at the convenience of your neighbor and his lawyer, and probably followed by a high tea in the law firm's paneled library. Forget that and hire the big-city firm that represents Duncan's corporation. We're protecting major investments here and will want the very best representation. Large city firms have rabid young lawyers available to serve on these matters, men and women who don't belong to the same clubs as your neighbors and who don't golf with them on Saturday afternoons. No gentlemanly restraint here—it's flaying time: full-metal-jacket, pedal-to-the-metal hardball, with depositions scheduled for the most inconvenient times in scruffy locations simply loaded with linoleum and nasty hard chairs, personal attacks on the defendant and his attorneys, and harassment of the highest order. In short, it's all-out war, and you're going to love it.

You didn't say whether your neighbor is a new arrival like yourself or a hanger-on from simpler times. If the latter, the first letter from your lawyers should hurry those peacocks off to the packing factory, because he'll never be able to afford the fight. If the former; if the bird fancier is one of our generation, than hang on to your hat and toss your wallet in the air: you're in for quite a ride, at $450 per hour. There's nothing more fun than a

–2–

full-fledged legal battle—a true suburban warrior never thinks twice about spending $150,000 to rid himself of a tree blocking his view, a boat stored during the winter under an ugly blue tarp, or someone's adamant refusal to mow his fields. At the risk of stating the obvious, there's no point having money if you can't (a) show it off and (b) use it to get your way. Sic 'im!